women caught in the
CROSSFIRE

women caught in the
CROSSFIRE

One Woman's Quest for Peace in South Sudan

ABUK JERVAS MAKUAC

&

SUSAN LYNN CLARK

Aristata Press

Library of Congress Control Number: 2023910827

Project Coordinators: Judy Blankenship and Anne McClard
Cover and Jacket Design: Anne McClard
Editor: Jenefer Angell

ISBN 978-1-7362316-7-8 (paper)
ISBN 978-1-7362316-6-1 (hardcover)
ISBN 978-1-7362316-6-1 (ebook)

The epigraphs at the beginning of each chapter are traditional African proverbs.

This book is a non-fiction account of the author's experience in which she remains
true to the facts as she remembers them. Her story describes and depicts the violence
of war and the hardships of being a refugee.

Aristata Press, Portland, Oregon
www.aristatapress.com

DEDICATION

To my family, especially my children, may this book inspire a great hope to never give up. To the countless men, women and children that we lost during the struggle for freedom. And to all the resilient women with whom I've worked to bring about peace to South Sudan.

CONTENTS

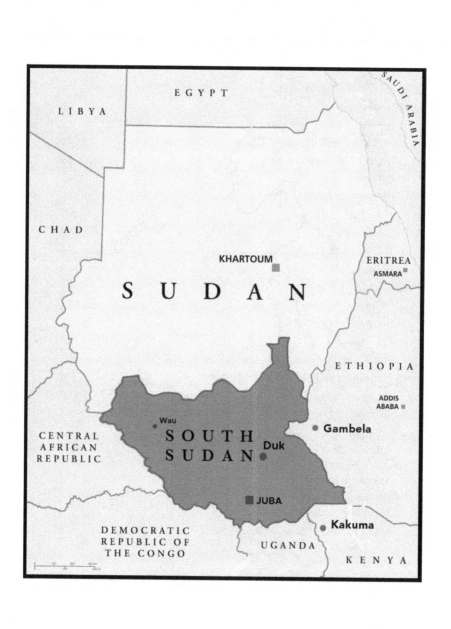

INTRODUCTION

It is September 2018. I have come to talk with Abuk in her daughter Sahra's apartment in Dallas. We will go over the text of her story again, and I plan to ask about her current work for unity and peace.

She comes out of the back room with tears in her eyes. When I ask if she is okay, she tells me, "Two great ladies died today. One died in Khartoum from old age, one was killed by her husband in Canada."

That day, I recorded her final thoughts about this book, its purpose, and its meaning to her:

All is struggle. I don't see that there is a good life in war. If there is a good life from it, it has taken great effort to get that better life. This is true for all of us, not me alone.

For all South Sudanese, in material things, there is nothing that our parents left for us. Fighting leaves nothing good for you to pass on to your children. Our only inheritance has been war.

So, you fall and try to lift yourself. All South Sudanese are like this. Our hope is that our children will learn to create something good for their offspring to build on. In exile in the West, my children have been learning this. And I am happy.

My generation grew up in war and our children were born into a war place. But we carried them out and brought them to a place with schools and with people who have lived in peace for generations. Now my grandchildren are born in a peaceful place.

When you see someone that's weaker than you, you cry in the name of that person. You will tell others what happened to them. I am writing a book that will be here even after I leave this world. It is a teaching book. People will read it and they will feel what war suffering can do to a people. They will tell the ones who are fighting to stop.

Let us not fight over religions either. Religion is something where you should sit down. There is a book of Christianity and a book of Islam and a book of the Jews. Let us hold to the wisdom that is in each book, not fight over which book it is in.

My grandfather is Muslim; he gave his daughter to a Christian man. And I, his daughter, became a Christian too. But my grandfather never said, Don't come to my house because you are a Christian. We ate together as one family, day after day: the same food at the same great table.

There is one rule to make peace: I let you talk and you let me listen to you. If you convince me, then I will join you. If not, do not kill me.

It is a simple rule.

War is not a good thing. I hope my words and my life will contribute to peace.

ABUK JERVAS MAKUAC AND SUSAN LYNN CLARK

ROAD TO ITANG

Fire does not give birth to fire, but to ashes.

"She's my wife and she'll go with me."

My husband stood up, silencing my father's protests that I might be killed along the way, daring to disrespect my father's wishes in my father's own domain. To the eye of a hawk, my homeplace in South Sudan may have been nothing more than a dusty heart beating slowly in the savanna, its red powder pulsing out through the grasses from the dirt roads where trucks, old cars, and cattle crisscrossed paths. But Wau was red-stoned and semiurban, too, the provincial capital since British rule. And my father's house was known here—the house of a Dinka police commander—British-style, with high stone walls crowned with glass shards to cut intruders. To my husband, now bent on civil war, this town and my father's place in it was unimportant, an impediment. But to me, a girl not yet twenty, it was my world.

But this is not when my trouble first began, when the earth first started to shift and wash away from under my feet like mud in sudden rains. It started some days before this one, on a day like any other, in 1984, in the third year of my marriage.

My husband, a man in his thirties, translator for the General Assembly, came home as usual to our bedroom in the great house. On this night, he did not remove his suit jacket and tie, unlace his shoes and lie back. He stood rigid by our bed and stared at me and our infant son—our second born. We had already lost one child, Bil, on the day of his first birthday.

It was not uncommon for Maker to come home angry. On those days I kept myself and Dut quite still. But the trouble in his face today was different, deeper, and though the tightness of his muscles was familiar, there was no smell of alcohol on his breath this time, no balling up of his fists. Today his anger was weighed down with fear and stillness.

"Abuk, I heard something this afternoon."

"What did you hear?"

I worked the wooden comb slowly through my little son's tight curls and waited. Maker was a small man whose words could make a leopard turn his spots to stripes, but his own mind could never be changed, not by anyone. But today, something in his tone was.

"We will talk later."

The late afternoon meal awaited us, spread on the veranda, bringing with it, as it always did, the familiar, wide embrace of my great family. Today my father, more fluent in English than Arabic, welcomed his brother-in-law along with his wives and a crowd of children and hungry young men. I came to the table now, starved for reassurance. The familiar carvings in the great legs of the table, the tiny antelope of polished wood stretching their necks above the shelves, the cool tile marbling the floor, the warm breath of slow-cooked bone and meat, the sting of *jibneh* cheese mixed with *fuul* had always had the scent of forever in them. But today, no matter how deeply I breathed, that sense escaped me. Broad bowls were emptied and then replenished as everyone's stomachs stretched. But mine, though also full, felt hollow.

A FEW HOURS AFTER THE LAST RINGING OF CHURCH BELLS, MAKER sent me to settle Dut and prepare for sleep. Our bed had been hand built by Hassan, a great craftsman in Wau. In those days Dinka and Arab mixed in trade and in the streets. Hassan had carved two lion heads into our bed's top section, and lion's feet as the bed's feet, gripping the floor with their curled claws. As I pulled back the floral coverlet, I felt Maker's eyes on me. I hadn't heard him come in, but there he was, sitting next to the open window.

At the last light of day, he slipped in quietly beside me and lay still. The warmth of his body was real and reassuring. Focus and strength had returned to him. I let myself feel safe. He began,

"Since the government in the North has become radical, Islamic, they've stopped listening to us in the South. We cannot tolerate it."

He stretched himself and put his hands behind his head.

"John Garang is the one man who can pull us together to fight this."

"John Garang?"

"He has the American PhD; he was a Sudanese army commander, but he has defected with his troops and will lead us."

"Lead us into what? Into a war?"

"Yes, war. Trouble has already started in the North. Some of my outspoken friends have disappeared. Some are in prison; others are dead."

I reached to take his hand, but it was clenched to the other behind his head.

"I'm sure my name is on their list, too. We will leave Wau soon."

I heard the night cry of large birds and a lion's low growl. In our town, the wild was still with us but caged in a zoo near our house. These animals came alive at night, especially before the change of seasons. They always felt it first and announced it to each other and to anyone who would hear.

"So, I will join Garang, and you and Dut will come with me."

An early childhood memory suddenly awoke in me and I hear people screaming. Gunshots behind me. Bullets flying past me. My feet can't find ground. My big brother Juma, my hero, calls me, my mother turns around and grabs us both and drags us running, slipping, struggling through the tall grass. It was Anyanya I, the first civil war.

"I can't go with you," I said. "Please don't take us to war."

Maker was up on his elbow now. "Take you to war? I have a chance at a scholarship in England. What if I told you we are going to England? Would that suit you?"

"Wau is my home."

"Your home is with me."

He laid back and turned away, the matter settled. His breathing slowed and deepened while mine did not. Meanwhile the lions carved in wood above us just stared as they always did, one facing the window, one facing the wall.

In the days that followed, I clung to fading guarantees of peace in life's routines. *Make tea and porridge at 5 a.m. Go to the market before 7, while the vendors still have the freshest things, before the liver and tomatoes are gone. Make breakfast for Maker at 9 a.m. Make dinner for everyone by 3. Put Dut to bed at 9.*

But in the morning the memories of that night rumbled like thunder across my mind, especially on the path to Souk Wau Market, a half hour from my home. This path held other memories, too. It was on this road where Maker's sisters had kidnapped me three years before. Before my other suitor knew anything, Maker, with their help, took me as his own. That was how things were done in those days. A girl could have her dream but a man would have his way. And now I had his child.

"Sister, good morning! Our mangoes are the best today! Come and buy!" *When will my husband make his next move?*

"No, ours are better! Come over here!" *Until then I will enjoy the duties of my days.*

The mottled colors of mango and lulu and bright pearl millet, deep purple eggplant, and the green chickpea spread out before me in the market. Colors called my eyes, and people called my name. In this place I was free to enjoy everyone, talk to anyone, free to choose what I would buy.

On the right, women sat in the smoke of sandalwood under acacia trees to perfume their bodies and soften their skin. On the left, the manly smell of fresh tobacco mixed with the dark breath of fresh goat soup and garlic, foretelling a rich lunch for the market's men.

Chickens squawked. Roosters crowed. Women bargained. Then I overheard two men arguing in the Dinka tongue.

"I am telling you, war is coming. We must join now." One of them was young, my age. The other was an older, well-dressed man.

"You are a fool to believe them," he said.

"It is in print, uncle."

"Put down that trash!" He tore the leaflet from the young man's hands. "We have abundant food. We have our schools and our businesses. I fought in the last civil war to gain this for us, and I will fight no more."

They separated and walked on, but I picked up the leaflet. Five hundred government troops stationed in the town of Bor had refused to return north. Col. John Garang was declared the head of this liberation army and was calling for others to join.

Those words walked with me on the long path home. This was the night that Maker planned to speak to my father. So I drank the song of every bird, like old wine, to dull my fears.

AT FIRST, HE ONLY SAID WE WOULD GO NORTH TO KHARTOUM. "IT IS their fault," he told my father. "It's the Islamists. They broke their word to us. They've cut the south up in three pieces and now hold to sharia law as an excuse to throw anyone in jail."

"Why start another war?" my father said. "Where will it end?"

"This will be a short fight. The government is unpopular, and the army itself is mad." My husband stood to end the discussion. "The decision has been made. We will go."

So, I packed everything I treasured, my best jewelry and clothes, my most expensive soaps and creams. But I could not pack my heart. It would stay behind in the arms of my family and in the fine markets of Wau.

A three-day, dusty train ride bore us north. These days, hundreds of others were going this way too, packed skin to skin in every train car, hundreds more on top. Our small family's spot was slightly better because of Maker's job but that did not stop the swirling dust from burning my baby's eyes, nor did it sweeten the stench of poorer travelers crammed like cattle, soaked with sweat, their children tucked like rags into every empty space. There was only one train north. On it, all travelers were equal.

Maker's cousin, a chief warden of the local prison, drove us from the train to an airport. A Russian Antonov bomber was waiting there to take almost a hundred of us on the last leg to Khartoum. The airport was no more than an old brick building, open on all sides, too small to fit so many people. Most carried big cloth bags, but we had a Samsonite suitcase from Britain. The northern army commander Abdel Hei was deciding who out of the hundreds could get on. It didn't matter who was first or last. If he didn't like something about you or if he thought you were a defector, he told you to get out of line.

He asked Maker, "Where are you going?"

My husband said, "My son is sick with tonsils. I'm accompanying my wife to Khartoum."

So the commander let us pass. The plane was open like a ballroom inside, with few seats, just ropes that swung. At first, the men took the seats and left no place for the women and children. Then Maker and another man asked them to stand and let the women sit. But even seated, I was holding Dut with one hand and a rope with the other. The runway was short, with broken concrete. The children cried as the plane jerked and threw us backward, shooting up to clear the trees. One month later we heard that John Garang's army had shot down a plane just like ours out of the sky.

We arrived in Khartoum with just enough money to get a flat the size of one bedroom in my father's house. The city was a dusty, squared-off desert of heartless buildings and nameless people. Soon after Maker was established as an officer in the movement, he invited his colleagues to eat with us.

That day, Maker was at his best. His compact stature and open smile made people put down their guard. He was the intellectual match of any man. I stood by him in a blue silk dress, bright with flowers, dark with leaves, and for this day I put on my gold rings and best arm bracelets. I served kisra and stew, rice and okra, English tea with milk, and boiled eggs for the children.

I asked one guest about life in Khartoum.

"It is hard." Deng, a member of the new Sudanese People's Liberation Army, answered me without hesitation.

"Hard?"

"Hard to get a job. Hard to get food. Hard to find a place to live."

Our apartment was small, but the community here was not. More guests than we'd invited were arriving.

Deng's wife asked, "Have you gone out much?"

I shook my head.

"Be careful."

"Why?"

"If the police find a woman talking with a man and she doesn't have their marriage certificate with her, she will be whipped."

"Whipped?"

"It's the law. And if you are accused of stealing, they cut off your hand."

I rubbed my wrists.

"I am telling you, give them no excuse to harm you."

I had cooked from early morning and had been very hungry before this, but no more.

"Abuk, talk to that woman over there. She has been in prison. She is from Wau too."

Lucia! I know her! She and her husband had left Wau before us. He was a government minister now.

"Lucia, how are you!" Our embrace enclosed her baby. I bent down to welcome the young girl beside her. "And this is your daughter? She must be six now!"

"Seven."

"She is beautiful! And your baby?"

"Nine months now."

"And how are you?"

We found space to talk in the kitchen. Her face was as tense as her fist as she struggled to open a small jar of sauce. "To tell you the truth, many things have happened to us here." I took the jar from her hands and emptied it into a small bowl, which disappeared into the hands of the guests.

"Abuk, we've had no money since we got here." Out of the corner of my eye I saw two boys by the window. The smaller one was the color of sand. The taller one was dark like me.

"The other Sudanese expect our help because my husband has a government job." The two boys were arguing over a piece of bread. "So we have many, many Southerners at our table. But we're as poor as they."

More people were arriving. I could see through the kitchen door that all the plates had only scraps now. Some guests came into the kitchen to help put out what more they could find. Then there was nothing more.

"I've been making alcohol at home and selling it to keep us alive. I throw incense onto the fire so that the smell will go away. I hide the pots. The police have come to search us many times. Twice they found evidence against me. Twice they put me and my newborn child in jail."

Lucia's daughter led us back into the main room. There, I saw my hungry guests with new eyes. Why hadn't I seen how worn their clothes were? What was I thinking when their eyes turned from my jewelry to their empty hands?

Lucia continued, "My best customers are the Islamic police. But did they help me when I was in jail? No. You can never trust them!"

"Abuk, I'm going out with Ngor and Lual." I hadn't noticed my husband standing at my side. He kissed me. "We have important business in town. I'll be back later." Concern for him and for my son was getting big inside me now.

"Everyone says you are an excellent cook!" he called back as he left with his close friends. The rest of the guests soon followed. By sunset the apartment was empty. Only my worries stayed behind to talk to me.

While Dut slept on the couch, I washed the pots and dishes, looking out again and again at Khartoum through the window. The pattern of the streets was foreign; the alleys were narrow and led to nowhere I could see. The lights in this part of the city were dim and revealed nothing I could name. I was lost, turning this way and that, alone in my thoughts, and then later, this way and that, alone in my bed.

As the days wore on in Khartoum, my husband grew more occupied with war. In late 1984 we moved to Cairo, though Maker at first had told me that we were going to England. Once in Cairo, we moved again and again within the city. As our residence changed from place to place, my husband's mind changed from plan to plan.

By day, he would say, "Tomorrow I'll send you to England, you and my son, to be safe." Then at night, when he had taken some drink and anger came up in him, he would tell me, "I will never send you there."

"But this morning you said...."

"I am much older than you. You will go to England and find a younger man."

"Believe me, I will not."

"I know your kind."

In Cairo is where I first learned to make my own mind small. If I looked only at the things in front of my eyes and cared for the things I held in my hands, my heart could stay calm.

Then finally one morning he said, "Pack your bags, Abuk. We're going to the airport."

I counted Dut's diapers and put them, one by one, next to his small traveling bag. Then I took his little shirts and shorts, still folded, from the place they had lain, for only a few days this time. I placed them on the bed to count them, then lost count and began to count again.

"What? You don't want to fly to England?"

I moved a little faster.

"Pack bags for me too."

It is morning. We are going together. We will fly to England. He will start his master's degree. We will have a house in London by his brother. I held my mind to these thoughts and placed my things and his into our bags.

2
ANOTHER CHANGE OF PLANS

Do not throw away your water simply because you
heard it will be raining.

WE ARRIVED EARLY AT CAIRO INTERNATIONAL. INSIDE THE TERMINAL, uniformed men shoved past me, as women with their children raced to catch up. Flags hung high, red-striped as meat on market day. The shifting smells of human sweat and jet fuel dizzied me to near intoxication. So I dreamed hard about flying across the Mediterranean and over Europe and then to England. To England, hilly and moist, populated with thick green gardens and laughing children. It will not be flat and dry like Egypt, not rough and dusty like Khartoum. I was there once before and I know.

In British streets, flowering trees grow quietly side by side with the people, just like in my hometown Wau.

My husband left me to my dreams and went to pick up our boarding passes. When he returned, his mood did not match mine. He sat watching the clock and watching me for a long time as I fed and cared for Dut. The look in his eye was alert, like the eye of a lion watching zebra, calculating which way the animal will leap when he springs. Eventually he spoke. "Abuk, we're going to resistance headquarters in Ethiopia."

Ethiopia? No!

"Everyone is there now."

Then trouble will be there too!

"It is a good place for us."

Before I could pull any words out of my throat, the boarding call came.

On the plane I found my tongue. "Maker, what's going to happen to us there?"

"Don't worry."

"Do we have enough money? What about Dut?"

"I have a hundred US dollars and I know people." He leaned back in his seat and closed his eyes. "You talk too much."

At times like this my stomach and my mind were one. They ached and cramped together. Before I could form a better thought, we were already stepping out onto the tarmac in Addis Ababa, and the warm air in my lungs was exchanged for cold. It was 20 degrees below what it was in Cairo. Whatever extra clothing I had, I wrapped around my son.

At baggage claim, a sand-colored man called out, "Maker!" and picked up our baggage, saying nothing more.

I rode in silence with them through the city. When the driver parked in front of the great Hotel D'Afrique, I whispered in Dinka to my husband, "We can't afford this."

The driver carried our luggage into the crowded, high-ceilinged lobby. I followed, carrying my little son. The well-dressed crowd parted slightly to make way. A broad, uniformed man in his mid-forties strode toward us with a dozen taller men around him—their faces stiff as wooden masks, their eyes darting up and down, taking pains to include every part of me in their inspection of the lobby. The great man extended his hand to Maker.

"Hello, *nasib!* Welcome!" He looked familiar.

"Kerubino! I am pleased to see you!" Maker said. I knew him—the commander himself, vice president of the liberation movement and leader of the liberation army! Seeing his face close-up, I remembered my father's hand, holding firmly onto mine. When I was fourteen, my father took me to Kerubino's village, to meet with some of our family there. On that day I stared into Kerubino's face, too, and my father squeezed my hand hard as the two of them argued bitterly. *How is it that now this man calls my husband "brother-in-law, nasib?"*

In the next breath, he turned to greet others. My husband turned quickly, too, loudly greeting more uniformed men. I stood behind him, dressed in silk, tall and still, holding my son.

In the next moments the crowd shifted toward the broad staircase. My husband went up, flanked by officers. A soldier my age approached me and then stood by in solitary kindness, his patience and his look indicating that I should go up with him.

Of all the questions in my mind, I asked him only the simplest one: "Where can I change my son?" He led me to the top of the stairs, to a small room there and waited again. I finished quickly and followed him, avoiding his eyes.

He led me into a great dining hall. Regimented tables set with plate, glass and silver, waiters bowing to the men already seated. The room was alive with flashing teeth, celebratory shouts, raised fists. A vacant chair awaited me, next to my husband, across the table from John Garang himself, the declared president of Southern Sudan.

"Madame, welcome to the Organization of African Unity," he said, extending his hand. His beard was speckled black and white like the back of a cormorant. He was not in uniform that day. In fact, all the seated men wore suits. Only the standing men wore uniforms here. Leaders were there from all over Africa. Garang was close friends with Mengistu Haile Mariam, President of Ethiopia, so he had been invited to the summit. He was lobbying hard at that time. But toward me he showed the sweet smile of an uncle.

Now noticed and welcomed, I felt comfort. Meeting and learning the names of military and political leaders like Dhol Acuil and Joseph Oduho, I felt secure. But in all of this great room I saw no other woman.

As the meal ended, Garang spoke quietly to my husband. "You will be leaving with a Sudanese from Germany and some others. A security guard goes with you. I wish you the best."

What happened next came very fast, as we were hurried out of the hotel. When our driver secured the doors to the Izuzu and quickly pulled away, I was still sucking the sweet taste of dill from between my teeth. My husband presented me and his son to the four men in the van: Commander Kerubino, a German Sudanese, the security guard, and another officer. Again I was the only woman. This time I did not ask even one question.

Once on the road, they pulled out German beer and soon they were feeling good. Kerubino asked me when my father was planning to come out here. "I don't know," I said, "We didn't tell him we were coming this way." Everyone who knew my father laughed. With Kerubino, the commander of the army in the van, what harm could come to us?

Soon we were passing through great mountains, miles outside of Addis. From the length of the shadows, it must have been late afternoon. When I caught sight of the sun, it was either on my right or just ahead, appearing now and then from between green slopes that were growing steeper and more rugged. The horizon stretched out behind them. Empty, vast, uninhabited. No sign of life or help as far as I could see. It was exhilarating and troubling.

"Pull over." Full of beer, the men decided to get out to pass water.

"We'll be back," they told the driver. "You look after the woman and the van."

The driver and I had drunk only water. We watched the officers disappear down an embankment behind us, hidden by tall grass. In silence, he and I waited inside the van on the empty road. Long minutes passed.

Slowly, slowly a rumbling and shaking crept up into the cab. Then we saw it, a low steel mountain grinding heavily toward us, filling the breadth of the road ahead. It stopped less than a rifle's length away, the muzzle of its gun aimed straight at us. Above its low growl only Dut's voice was heard, playful, crying. "Mama, Mama, big truck! I want it!" I covered his mouth and held him, his excited heart pounding next to my fearful one.

When I turned to find my husband, I saw armed soldiers leaping out of military vehicles coming up now from behind as well. They were running toward us with their rifles aimed, shouting orders at us in a language I could not understand. The driver and I faced forward and made ourselves small inside the van. In the side mirror I saw my husband and Kerubino, followed by the other two, scrambling up the cliff beside the trucks. They froze when they saw the rifles. Everyone froze. The soldiers motioned for my husband and the others to come forward and stand by the van.

Our security guard stepped toward them with his hands up. He tried to talk to them Ethiopian to Ethiopian, but they would have nothing of it. He translated to Kerubino. "The soldiers want to see our departure order. But I don't have it."

Kerubino shouted at him, "What's wrong with you?"

"I just left it because I always have my national ID. Don't worry, they will let me pass, and there will be no problem. It will be okay."

But when the guard showed them his ID, they rejected it, too. The soldier rebuking him had his pistol aimed and ready. They didn't know who we were and they weren't going to accept anything our guard was saying. I felt guns trained on me on every side. But I kept thinking, "Kerubino is here...."

The soldiers ordered the men back into the van. The tank turned slowly and led us, while the military trucks closely followed, onto a winding dirt road that led down, down past the last thicket of trees, down deep behind the sheer cliffs, opening out onto a grassless field, into a wild spider's web of deeply rutted tire tracks, high rusted fencing as far as I could see, lines of artillery, and then beyond that, a boiling pot of men and trucks and rolling guns aimed upwards at the sky.

They stopped us at the gate, where soldiers, more than I could count, surrounded us again.

My husband was boiling too, "These people, they don't know what they're doing."

"They are going to kill us," I whispered.

"Shut up."

One of the soldiers approached the van and yanked the door open and ordered the security guard out. They dragged him by the neck into one of the huts.

By now it was about seven o'clock. Kerubino was becoming

agitated. The muscles of his neck and shoulders tightened as he moved his hand to the door. Our driver gripped the wheel to control his own shaking and pleaded, "Please, sir, don't make a move. Everyone, please just remain calm." Our driver knew these people.

The soldiers looked well trained and confident, each with a pistol holster and a handheld machine gun. Hours passed, and it became evening. We had no news of the security guard, no water, no word from anyone. My father's words were going through my mind, "If you go to war with Maker, you will be killed—or worse."

It had been all day since I'd passed water. I'd been shifting this way and that inside the van for hours, uncomfortable, growing desperate, but afraid. But now the pain was unbearable.

The driver called softly to one of the guards to communicate this. The guard came close enough to study me. He smiled and got another soldier. They motioned to the others, then took me out and walked me to a tree in the open yard and pointed to the ground. They were going to watch me, both of them, all of them. With his rifle ready, the first soldier pulled a box of cigarettes out with his left hand and flipped it open with his thumb. He pulled a cigarette out with his teeth and smiled and said a few words to the other man. I watched them out of the corner of my eye, not knowing what they were planning. I had to force myself to do what I had to do with their eyes on me. The first soldier took a long drag and let the smoke out of his mouth into the air. All the while, they watched, not even pretending to look away. When I finished, the first soldier put his cigarette out and spoke to the other one, laughing.

Now Kerubino got mad. He started cursing and yelling inside the van, "These idiots, do they even know who I am? I'll have all of them thrown into prison!" A soldier standing by said something to the driver and made a threatening gesture with his gun. The driver spoke to Kerubino, "Please, sir, calm down. If you get mad, they will get bad with you."

Regardless, Kerubino lost control. He pulled out a pistol and opened his door. The driver screamed, "Sir, please don't do that!"

Soldiers quickly raised their rifles and aimed them at Kerubino's head. He put the pistol down. An officer shouted something at the driver.

Kerubino shouted back, "Tell him I must talk to General Masfin!"

The officer studied Kerubino as the driver translated his answer, "He says no one can talk to Masfin."

Keeping his rifle aimed at Kerubino, the officer radioed back. Then a higher-ranking officer came up and spoke to Kerubino directly, in English, "Give me the names of everyone in the car, starting with you."

The first officer lowered his rifle and shoved paper and pen into the driver's hand. Kerubino wrote down all our names, including my son's, and handed it over. Another soldier took the paper and left while the commanding officer stayed. The soldiers continued to surround us, rifles aimed.

Within ten minutes a soldier came running back. He spoke to the commanding officer, who opened our car door respectfully and spoke to us in a low voice. "General Masfin says you must be released." He shouted over his shoulder a few words in his language, and the soldiers lowered their guns.

Suddenly we were all let out of the van to straighten our backs and breathe. Dut clung to me. It was dark by now. The commanding officer tried to explain, "You need to know this was nothing personal." But then he lowered his voice to a growl and looked straight into Kerubino.

"But, sir, next time do not pull out your gun. Because if someone shoots at me, I will shoot him and all the people with him."

While he was talking, another soldier came, half dragging, half carrying our security guard from the hut where they had taken him. His face was swollen, his lip cut deep, and blood soaked his clothes. He needed three men to help him into the car. We cleaned him up as much as we could and, thanking God, drove out of the camp.

The poor man was shaking and crying—tears flowed in place of the blood we'd wiped from his face.

We got back on the road, going fast now.

"I work for my country, and my fellow soldiers treat me like this. I don't want this job. I don't want this life."

He pushed open the door to jump out. Kerubino caught his jacket and held him. As we pulled off the road, the others got control of him and put him in the seat between me and my husband. We held him there as we drove on.

"Don't talk like this. You need to live," we told him. After a while, his voice weakened, and he leaned forward into his hands, with no more strength to weep.

All I wanted to do now was to find a safe place to put my child to sleep and lay my own body down next to his. By late evening, we reached Nazaret. The driver took us first to John Garang's residence there, where we had been expected for dinner long before. In the moonlight, I could see it was a large house with a flowering garden.

I was too nervous to eat. Dut was crying, so I walked up and down the hallway, carrying him and calming myself while the others dined. My husband talked and laughed with them. Before midnight, the driver came back to take us on.

As I climbed back into the dusty van, I smelled the army camp again and felt the soldiers' eyes on me. When we pulled away from the house, the moon followed us like a searchlight as I held Dut close by my locked door. Each time I drifted off I dreamed a soldier was staring in at me through the dirty window.

We arrived at the Adan Aras Hotel after midnight but my husband and I lay awake until dawn. The baby was agitated, too. I rocked him gently as we talked.

"Why did they beat our security guard so badly?"

Maker breathed deep and stretched himself, "I don't know."

"But he was one of them...." The ceiling fan turned slowly. "Do you really think we're safe here?"

"I don't know." Maker put his arm around me. "But I trust Garang." I felt my husband's heart beating slowly, steadily. It calmed mine. Towards dawn, we finally fell asleep.

I don't know what time it was when we rose. The sun poured into the room and called us to the window to look out. What a pretty place they'd brought us to. There were old, broad trees, rambling gardens, and so many different blossoms— yellow, white, red. I saw birds flitting from tree to tree, feathered bright yellow, summer green and crimson, singing so many different colored songs. I loved this hotel immediately. There was nothing ugly here.

A knock came at the door. Other Sudanese exiles had come to join us. "Good morning! Good morning!" We embraced them and welcomed them in and called room service.

"Who speaks Amharic well?"

Two or three said they knew a few words.

"Who can read this menu?"

No one.

So, though our stomachs growled for everything we imagined on the menu, we only knew how to ask for a bowl of boiled eggs. An army general and his wife, and the chief of staff and his wife were with us. Even Awut Deng, a woman from my hometown, was here. Everyone was asking us about people we'd left behind. All were telling stories of their dangers on the road.

Day after day, our number grew. I was the youngest, but my shyness melted away as I told them the fear I felt in the mountains, the anger I felt toward the men that beat the guard, how I worried for my son. They repeated my story to newcomers. Everyone shared my fears. Very soon I felt myself part of them.

I had never felt this kind of strength before: accepted into a circle of power, bound with them in the simplest and the greatest things, swept up into something larger than myself. I felt I could face both life and death by the side of these people. Now I understood my husband's allegiance and the purposes of war. Those few days in that hotel were the highest days of my life.

ON THE SEVENTH NIGHT THEY TOLD US, "MAKER AND ABUK, YOU will leave tomorrow for Itang. The SPLA has arranged everything. You will have a house there."

I was full of anticipation. The officers' homes in Nazaret were shaded and beautiful.

But that evening my cousin Awut took me aside, "Abuk, before

you go you must get as much soap and skin cream as you can carry."
The men told Maker to buy a mattress. These instructions did not
make sense.

It was a pleasant first day of October, a mix of gray and white
clouds, but I felt the sky was longing to release a heavy weight of
rain. We traveled by bus, reaching Gore at the end of the first day.
There we met some Sudanese men traveling from Itang back to Addis
for military training. We asked them about the Sudanese in Itang.
They said only a little.

"Yes, so-and-so is there" or "So-and-so's uncle is sick" or "So-
and-so's wife will have a baby." As they spoke, I pictured Itang as a
place where Sudanese gathered to live a traditional life in a foreign
land until the war would be over—a place with open markets and
sprawling houses to welcome the ever-growing, reuniting families.

In Gore we exchanged vehicles with the men and were loaded
into their truck—an eight-wheeler with loosely fitted railings rattling
above the truck bed as we drove. The front seat held three people:
the driver, and the wife of the chief of staff, and her daughter in her
lap. Maker, Dut, and I and a Sudanese man from Kenya, his wife
and five children with him, sat on suitcases in the back of the open
truck.

As we drove higher and higher up into the mountains, cold wind
cut into our eyes, and tears poured out. We used bed sheets to protect
ourselves and wrapped blankets around our children. As the road
narrowed to nothing more than a jagged scar carved up and across the
face of great cliffs, the truck swerved, leaning left and right. Maker
never once opened his eyes. I sat trembling against the slats. But the
man from Kenya joked, "Don't worry. If this truck falls from here, it
will take it three days to hit bottom. That gives us plenty of time to
get out!"

After an eternity, we arrived in Gambela, our last stop on the road
to Itang. It was a gray and simple town, soaked by days of rain. The
market there had everything.

"You want a mattress? I find you the best." The local seller was
friendly, an Arabic speaker.

"How much?"

"For you, not too much. You travel with your family, no? Go eat. I'll put the mattress on the truck for you."

Maker was the first to lie back on the mattress once we were on the road again. But then he sprang up and got on his hands and knees. He poked his fingers around its center and its side. He tried to turn it. It was very heavy.

"Something's wrong here."

He took a knife and slashed it open. Plastic things, dirty rags and trash bubbled up from the long cut, along with a smell like meat on its sixth or seventh day.

Maker cursed Gambela and made the driver stop. He, the driver, and the Kenyan man tugged and heaved the mattress out, leaving it to rot by the side of the road.

"We'll buy a better one in Itang," I said. Maker turned away.

So I leaned back with my son against the wooden railings, grateful that we were still alive and at last out of the mountains and now passing through the southern valley. I was soon lulled to sleep by the deep vibrations of the laboring engine and the closeness of my little boy. The hard boards of the truck bed, the slats of the tall sides fell away in my sleep. I felt myself floating in the high-ceilinged hotel of Nazaret, inhaling the sweet flowers of the walkways, hearing the birds that sang in the morning.

We hit a hole in the road, and I woke suddenly, not sure now where we were.

Across from me, my husband was still rigid, looking out the back, impatient. The tension of his face, the squint of his eyes, told me he was still arguing in his mind with the man who sold him the mattress. I raised my arms to the sky and breathed in. I could smell wet earth, around us splashing sounds were getting louder, water droplets leapt into the truck from the road. The others in the back were dozing still: the tall man from Kenya with his wife still dressed well from the farewell at the hotel, their five children quiet, disciplined, and my Dut curled up, sweet and trusting, not yet three years old.

Through generous openings between the slats, the late afternoon sun, having dropped down now below the clouds, shared its light with us inside the truck. My dress, so much admired at the hotel, was now

limp and badly wrinkled. *I will iron it as soon as we get there.* I felt
my son squirm, restless in my lap.

The road narrowed. As we rounded a curve, I saw an odd building, out of place with its long tin roof and broad United Nations
insignia. A blue flag hung limp like laundry after a rain. Our truck
slowed down. Soon we were surrounded by very thin people walking
on this side and on that, along the road, across the road, behind us,
looking in. There were scattered tents. Straw huts squatting in the
mud. Water—muddy water—everywhere, and in the midst, our
raised, narrow stretch of road. We now came to a stop. There was a
thick smell in the air, the smell of dead animal.

I called to the driver. "How much farther?" Mosquitoes were
drifting in and sitting on Dut's little arms. "Please drive on! It's
getting late. We need to get to Itang."

The driver turned and shouted, "Sister, we *are* in Itang!" He
jumped down from the cab and slammed the door.

The hairs on the back of my neck stood up. Before I could say
anything more, my husband and the Kenyan man jumped down to
join him. I had no choice but to lower myself and Dut down from the
truck bed, too. When my feet touched the road, a crowd of black
skeletons enclosed me,

"Welcome, how are you?" They stretched out their thin hands.
"Will you be staying here?"

Their skin hangs from their bones like rags.

"Where are you from? Have you heard, is anyone still alive in
Bohr?"

*How can they stand and speak with no flesh to pull their bones
together?*

"Do you have any news from Juba?"

They study me and squeeze my hands. I must answer.

"No, I don't have any news.... Yes, I am also from Wau.... No,
we didn't walk out of Sudan. We flew from Cairo."

They speak Dinka like me.

Suddenly among them, I saw the face of my brother-in-law! But
when I stepped off the road to greet him, my foot sank into something
that had the innocent look of wet dirt. I sank, not just to the ankle or

up to the calf, but to the knee, then to the thigh, in murky, mud-mixed water. Dut cried out, "No, no. Not going in!" I caught him and held him higher on my hip. I reached in and pulled off my shoes and raised my dress to save what I could of it. Still close to the truck, my husband pulled off his own shoes and socks and rolled up the cuffs of his suit pants.

His half-brother called to us both to follow, "It's the rainy season here."

The people who had come to welcome us, as thin as they were, were strong. Two of their men pulled our bags from the truck and swung them above the water and onto their heads. They followed my brother-in-law slowly through the flood toward a raised cluster of small huts.

"Brother-in-law," I called. "In Nazaret they told us that we would have a house in Itang. Where are the houses?"

He looked at Maker for permission and then said to me, "What you see is what there is."

There were only leaning tents and misshapen huts of mud and straw rising up from the earth like ant hills, some with stones and dirt packed round them, some encircled by watery ruts, draining hope from life. The long aluminum-roofed building to the left was standing on higher ground, its flag only slightly brighter than the gray sky that stretched out thick over the expanding hordes of stick people and their children. We were here to join them.

I turned to see my husband's face.

"Abuk, you need to understand. No one cares about this valley. No armies are going to fight over a place like this. Believe me, you and Dut will be safer here than anywhere else in the world."

3
LIFE IN A DEATH PLACE

When the lion cannot find meat, it eats grass.

OVER MAKER'S SHOULDER I COULD SEE THE SUDANESE MAN FROM Kenya gesturing forcefully to his unhappy wife.

My brother-in-law's two huts were just ahead, equally rough and dull, roofed with grasses now soaked in the rain. The men who had gone on before us with our things stepped up first and then bent low to place our bags inside the smaller hut. The spongy ground under my feet tilted up toward them. I clenched my toes and teeth to climb and not slide back. The older porter quickly took my hand.

"Thank you, uncle. Where do you stay?" I asked him.

"Sometimes here. Sometimes there. My family is not with me."

"I hope they will join you soon."

"No, I will join them." His soft voice and eyes carried in them the hope of death.

Ajwong's wife called out from the doorway of the bigger hut. "Abuk, your little boy is beautiful! How fat he is!" Two children stole looks at us from behind her with their big eyes set in hollow cheeks. "Greet your Auntie Abuk!" she said. They stepped forward, right hands reaching politely to touch ours, their hands as dry as lizard backs.

Now Ajwong swelled his chest and spoke to my husband. "We have been here a while now and are doing well. We've already built this second hut. It is yours till you can build one. We made other preparations for you, too!" The sweep of his arm enclosed a cooking fire and a pot that swung above it.

"Thank you, brother. May we unpack our things first?" My husband guided me toward the small, dark world of the second hut.

Through its doorway, I saw cooking tools piled in a far, dim corner. Along the left wall was a low, squared-off block of earth, the length of a man's body, the width of two, solidly joined to the clay floor, with a stiff grass mat and a flowered bed sheet spread on top. Another smaller, chair-like block grew up immobile from the clay of the floor on the right. I stared in through the doorway at both, my hands locked on my hips, my feet as fixed to the ground as my new furniture.

Dut pulled at my dress. "Mama, I'm thirsty." I looked around at the pale light of the weakening day reflecting itself in the flooded camp. "Mama, Mama!" He tugged at me. "I want Pepsi." Ajwong's wife laughed behind me and held out a tin cup, but Dut said, "No water! Pepsi!" So she invited him into their hut and made him boiled tea with a little powdered milk. He drank it and slept. I bent down and entered our new hut in silence. My husband was already stretched out on the mat. "Not bad," he said.

AROUND NINE OR TEN O'CLOCK, AJWONG CALLED OUT, "COME JOIN us for stew!" It was so dark by now we couldn't see what we were eating. I tasted salt in tepid water and felt a little bit of oil. Some threads of meat slipped past my teeth and down my throat. *What kind of stew is this?*

Ajwong heard me thinking in the dark. "What you are eating is our best. Enjoy it. You won't be having meat again for a while."

My husband admired the salty water, "Thank you, brother. It is great." I put my spoon down slowly.

It was easy to lie down after that. My body surrendered fear to weariness and made no more demands on me. The mat on our clay bed crackled as we turned, smelling of fresh cut grass; the sheet on top was stiff and bittersweet with strong soap. Soon my husband was as deep in sleep as my son. I drank my tears alone.

Long before the day would break, my stomach was already up and aching. I felt my way to the door, sick, restless, seeking light. But outside I was as blind and hopeless as inside. No moon. No stars. If there were clouds, there was no sun to make them either white or black. If there was still a camp, its drabness and its horror were both gone. The thick air shook with the song of insects and the low, irregular growl and caw of the bush. I fell asleep there, my back leaned up against the mud wall, hoping, hungry, waiting for a new day to give me back my sight.

A rasping, scraping sound awoke me. The sun straight into my eyes now, I was blind again, but colorfully. I heard voices and splashing, and—squinting—I saw movement inside a hut across from me. It took only a few steps through shallow water to reach there.

Through the low hut door I saw the flowered hem of a faded dress swish back and forth with every scraping sound. I bent down to look in and saw a young woman, just my age rubbing the wall of her hut, making big circles with her hands.

"Hello?"

She turned, surprised, and when I saw her face, my heart jumped up. "Habsa?" My classmate three years ago in Wau! Smart and strong and so much fun.

"Abuk!" Her hands were mud-caked and swollen, her face gaunt, but her smile was big, and her arms opened wide as she stepped outside to greet me.

"Shee-bok!" [How are you?]

"Shee-bok!" As we embraced, she held her muddy hands up and away from me.

"Habsa, is it really you!?"

"Yes, and God has brought you safely!"

We both cried.

"You escaped. Where is your baby boy?"

"In there, sleeping."

"So late?"

"Is this your own hut?" I asked. "Why are you thin like this?"

"I am all right. Did your father come with you?"

"No. Where is your husband, Habsa?"

"Away. Did you bring soap with you?"

Habsa dipped her hands in a water tub and rubbed them hard on a rough cloth. "I heard that you and Maker might come but I didn't want to shock you, letting you see me like this." She picked at a light spot on her forearm; it peeled off.

"What are you doing?" I asked her.

"Polishing our walls." She took a critical look at her work and another look at me. "You have to give them a fresh coat of mud every few months and polish them hard if you want to keep the snakes out."

I followed her eyes toward a line of brush. *How many snakes were outside my hut last night?*

"In rainy season you can do the inside of the hut, but the outside has to wait."

The skin of her hands was as rough as the walls and the grinding stone on the ground behind her. Seeing such stones in picture books and in my grandmother's village had always fascinated me. Seeing my friend's hands, I saw no romance in these stones now.

The stronger light of day showed hundreds and hundreds more huts and tents, with thousands more cooking pots and pans swinging from poles like half-mast iron flags. The same number of women, scattered near and far, were straightening their backs in the early morning, raising water jugs to their shoulders and then to their heads or reaching up to hang their sun-bleached clothes.

"Did no one tell you about life here?"

I took a deep breath and, with it, held my reeling thoughts in.

"Then I will tell you."

She wrapped her hands in the hem of her dress and, cradling a simmering pot, filled two tin cups with steaming tea-leaf water. A sweet scent rose from them, faint and seductive, like memories of home.

*Abuk (right) in Addis Ababa, Ethiopia with the late
Elizabeth Aguek Mangok, December 1986*

"Do you see those four huts? Those are four more households."

Water stood in pools between them. Each hut had its own stretching woman, its own smoldering fire, its own collection of tubs and tools and groggy children. The women seemed busy enough with their morning things, but I felt their thoughts on me.

"We put our work and our money together."

What good is money in a place like this?

"The five of us have become friends." I sipped the weak tea. Then drank. There was sweetness in it! *Where in this hell did she find sugar?*

"Habsa, I want to see the rest of the camp."

"You're not ready."

"I want to know where I am."

"No, you'll stay with us in the circle for now. It's better, at first."

MY HUSBAND WAS SOON GONE FROM US DURING THE DAYLIGHT hours, passing his time with UN officials and Sudanese leaders.

"It is a new camp and is growing too fast," he told me. "It was laid out for ten thousand refugees. Six times ten thousand have already come. The number of both the living and the dead is growing every day. There are decisions to be made, plans to be drawn up." I understood the situation but wondered where in this camp he found the alcohol I smelled on his breath every evening.

In the first days, women I didn't know brought small gifts of boiled maize for Dut. He seemed happy enough to eat from their hands and run and play with the other children. But since that first night, I could take only tea and, as advised, I did not step away from the five-hut circle.

"In this camp some people are hardworking, but some people after a time just give up. Then death comes." This was my third day with Habsa. "But the sky is clear today. I will take you around now, if you want to go." Dut was busy with Ajwong's boys. It was safe for him to stay behind.

"There's water everywhere. Rub this cooking oil on your feet and legs. Cover them thickly. It will protect you from what's in the water."

As we walked, Habsa greeted everyone. "Some days I work at the distribution tent. Some days at registration. They need people like us who can read and write."

A man's stiff body lay whitening by a tree in the open sunlight. *Was this his tree? He lies exposed. Is there no one to cover him, to give him rest?*

Habsa's eyes followed mine. "It is very sad, Abuk. It takes a lot of energy to bury the dead. The men of the camp must decide every day if they will use their strength to bury or to build. There is not enough for both."

We passed another man sitting up, staring at a blackened pot.

"His wife passed away. And as a man he doesn't cook."

"Do you cook for him then?"

"We offer him what we've made, but he always tells us he's just eaten."

"Why does he say that?"

The man's eyes tracked our passing.

"They say he doesn't want to eat now anymore."

She turned and walked toward a stretch of bush and tall grass.

"Let me show you the way to the river." She looked back at me. "Are you all right?"

"I'm all right."

We came to a place beyond the latrines, away from the huts, to the part of the river that bubbled with familiar sounds of play and gossip —the place for bathing the children and filling water jugs. By now, with the help of two days of sun, the floodwater was going down and the land was showing more of its shape and its contents.

"Be careful as you walk now. Keep your eyes open. But a little bit, try to keep them closed, too. Sometimes, if you see a hand or foot or head, it is just what happens when the flood comes and the shallow graves open. It's ok. Just turn away. The men will find them."

Oh, my stomach now was troubling me. Hungry, but loath to eat, it was closing up fast, deciding to not even drink water from a river so close to the dead.

Habsa felt me slowing down. "All right, this is enough for one day. Let's go back and have some food."

O God, I cannot eat.

"I have maize and a little milk."

"Milk, where there are no cows?"

"They call it milk, but it's a powder made from beans. We mix it with water. For us Dinka, it is really hard to drink it. But I have learned."

Habsa walked me back to Nyjang, Ajwang's wife. She had been waiting for us. She looked at me closely.

"You have taken her to the river, haven't you?"

"Only a short time."

"Are you all right?" She saw my right hand guarding my stomach.

"Yes." *But my head pounds and my stomach and my spirit both want to leave my body.*

"Come in and eat. You will feel better."

"Thank you." Ashamed to resist her kindness, I ate and, as long as

I stayed with her, I held the "milk" and corn mash down. But by nightfall, I felt I had swallowed a meal of knives. Every way I turned they cut me deeper. I cried until I vomited. I vomited until the last small knife was out of me.

More and more it seemed I was sleeping fewer hours than the sun. Today, I rose early and went out to find it. As I suspected, it still lay dozing in a golden sleep on the horizon, gathering its strength to make the steep climb into the sky. Then I thought I caught the smell of meat cooking. *Can it be?* But a sudden turn of the morning air covered everything again with the smell of wet, aging beans.

The only light that shined this time of day was from pre-dawn fires. The women of my circle were already gathered at Nyjang's fire, making tea and making plans. I did not know this predawn part of their routine. Habsa saw me and called me over.

They looked up at me and looked long at one another, then continued. Nyjang was speaking, "Habsa, today you will go for the water."

Habsa nodded. Then Yom, a young woman my age, spoke up, "Auntie Nyjang, I will go today to meet the woman with the cow."

The woman with the cow?

"Very good, and while you are both gone, I'll watch the children and grind maize."

There are cows here? There is milk for Dut?

"Abuk, you may go with Habsa, to get water."

Then I spoke up, "Thank you, Auntie Nyjang." I paused to gauge their trust of me, then asked, "But who is this woman with a cow? I've heard no talk of milk, except for this gray powder that's made from beans."

"You don't know? Ah yes, no one has told you—no one has known if we could trust you, being from the outside, being close to the command." They paused now, too, communicating together in silence.

"Told me what, auntie?"

"That if you have money, you can buy things." The air brightened.

Habsa opened her left hand. "Abuk, we have decided to make you part of the circle now." She held out two *birr* coins, about the value of twenty cents.

"There is money, but not everyone has it. If people know you have it, someone might take it, but if you have money you can buy a few extra things. And we have found a way to get it."

Now I was learning something. These women were not living like prisoners of war.

Habsa began, "Did you not notice this?" She pointed to a strange thing built out of pots and pipes and cloth set up behind her hut. "In bad times we make beer and sell it. You can do it too, if you want."

I had grown to hate alcohol and anything associated with it. "I have money left from our travels," I said. "I won't be needing to make beer!"

The women laughed and rolled their eyes.

Dut woke up while we were talking and ran from the hut with his arms open wide, "Mama, Mama!" I caught him up. "I'm hungry."

"So, is there a market, too?" I said.

"No. Just a few Ethiopians we can trust who live in a village up the river. When they hear we have money, they set aside milk for us. Or they kill a goat on a day when more women come up from the camp to buy."

"What about the camp people who have no money?"

"The new arrivals sell their clothes, if they brought any good things with them. Our Ethiopian neighbors love three things: beer, pretty clothes, and gold."

"You arrived here dressed well, didn't you? Perhaps you also have more in the suitcase you carried. You brought some nice clothes with you, didn't you, Abuk?"

"But I won't sell them. I can't. Maker said we are going back to Addis soon."

The women stole looks at each other, but no one said a word more.

Yom broke the silence. "Auntie Nyjang, let Abuk go with me to the cow woman."

"Yes, and find her an empty bottle too. If she has money, then let her buy."

That night I ate and kept my food down for the first time in seven days. I boiled the small cut of goat meat they'd shared with me and gave some with a little cow milk to Dut. Maker ate elsewhere with the men, but Dut and I dined well too that night and slept full.

From that day on, I was part of the cooking circle. Some days I walked to the river to carry water, some days I walked beyond the river to bring milk. Some days it was my turn to rise before everyone and make watery tea and then stay back for the first few hours of the day to watch the children and grind maize.

We boiled water together, washed clothes together, boiled milk, cooked, and talked and talked together. When one of us fell weak or sick, the others would do her part until she got up again.

I do not mean to say that there was enough food. No. Nor do I mean to say that it was easy to walk so far, to carry slippery jugs filled with heavy, wildly swinging water, or to grind rough corn against rough stone. I don't mean to fool you into thinking that we didn't wake up a little weaker every day or that we didn't see each other and our children growing thinner instead of fatter before our eyes.

All I mean to tell you is that we put our little strengths and hearts together, and, when added up, they equaled the strength and heart of one healthy woman. During the time when we worked together, we grew thinner, but not one person— man, woman or child—in our circle of families died.

4

NO, IT'S NOT WEDDING DAY

If you can't solve problems in peace, you cannot solve them in war.

SO IT WAS FOR MANY DAYS, AND EVERY DAY BROUGHT WITH IT A NEW grief and a new lesson.

When the rainy season reached its second peak, fish and baby crocodiles were swimming freely among our huts. And the sandy resting places of the dead, who only months before were placed in shallow graves dug with great effort by weakened men, dissolved. Those bodies now were jostling free, being lifted up by swirling water. And with them rose the scent of another world—dark sulfur mixed with fear.

But some things did not move. There was an outhouse, by our huts, and I thanked God for it. It was tall, more than a man, and an arm's length and a half across. Though its color matched the drab clay of the camp, it was made of flat wood and metal braces brought from overseas. It rose square, straight at the edges, like my pride.

One day, urgent to relieve myself, I left Dut and ran to it, splashing water high, pulling my feet out of sinking mud by the sheer force of forward movement. The rain was pouring. I passed a few dry moments inside that private place, the door shut, the world away, enjoying the music of rain's thick fingers drumming on thin wood, when suddenly my heart became uneasy. *Quickly, quickly*, it told me. *Get out now.* I left the outhouse open and ran back to the archway of my home and stayed there looking out and wondering why my heart had become so suddenly uneasy. *How beautiful the rain. It clothes the camp in silk, fills it with mirrors. How silent all but the rushing, swirling, silver rain.*

Then I saw the outhouse lean heavily to the left. Next, with a shift in undercurrent, it twisted dizzily to the right. I held my breath until at last it steadied itself a moment, like a grazed and stubborn soldier sets himself upright to be shot again. That's when the hollowed ground it stood on opened up, and my heart stopped. That's when it was sucked perfectly and vertically down.

What if I had been in there? Who would know? If someone knew, would they care? If they cared, who would jump in after me?

My hiding place had become a standing coffin—but my heart had warned me. So I decided to trust the warnings of my heart more than anything else in the world and resolved never to let myself be alone for too long again.

Maker's half-brother waited many, many days for us to build our own hut and move out of his. I say "us," because I felt ashamed, not because I was the one who was supposed to build the hut but because one of us had to feel ashamed. When two months had passed and the rains had long stopped, and the sun was out for building, Ajwong himself and his cousin came together to talk to my husband. While making tea for them I heard their talk over the play of children.

"Do you plan to build a place of your own soon, brother?"

"Yes, but you know I am not a builder." My husband, though a normal height among the UN workers, was short among tall Southern Sudanese. Even so, he could rule them by his words.

"You have been here for some time now." Ajwong's cousin, seated on a smooth stone next to Maker, had a gentle touch in his voice, but his eyes did not turn left or right from a man when he spoke to him.

"But I have barely passed any time in this compound. You know my work among the commanders."

"Everyone knows," Ajwong assured him.

"The commanders have many things to manage. All my days are spent with them in this."

"Yes, we respect you for it," Ajwong continued. "But, to be honest, brother, some people are worried that there is also concealed work going on."

Maker's voice dropped. "What are you talking about?"

"They say the commanders are also fattening young recruits on the UN food." Ajwong was an honest and direct man. I had also heard these things.

Maker had been twisting a thin branch with its leaves while they talked. Now it snapped in his hands. "Brother, this is not being done. Do you see anyone fat here?"

"No. And we are not saying we believe this." Ajwong's cousin softened the matter. "It is only what some people say."

"It sounds like empty talk from empty stomachs." Maker let the branch fall and dusted off his hands.

"Not everyone understands your work," Ajwong said. I was confused, too, even though I was his wife. In public, he inspired men with soft words of reason, talk of history and courage, but at home he spoke in anger—anger that we had been supplanted, anger that our social progress was again being interrupted, anger that the Southern Sudanese were again betrayed by the Arab "treaty-breakers" in the North. An anger that sometimes turned toward me as well.

Maker answered his half-brother calmly. "Everyone can see that here in the camp the commanders order and organize the neighborhoods. We help facilitate food distribution. We make note of the sick and dying. We serve the community."

"So you commanders are making peace instead of war?"

Maker shot an impatient look at me and at the heating water. I began to pour tea quickly, whatever the temperature.

"Our only goal is peace."

Ajwong's cousin shifted. "We just came here to help you in your living situation. We are concerned that it may not give a good impression to the people that your wife and son are staying this long in another man's hut." I felt suddenly afraid that the tension in the air was because of me. Was it not my and my son's fault that the men had come to him?

They rose to leave.

Maker challenged them. "Shall I stop the progress of war for the sake of a hut?"

"Now you talk of war?" Ajwong stopped and let the silence speak.

Before I could put their tea on the tray, the two men stood, turned, and left.

Maker stood quickly, too, dusting off his pants and adjusting the buttons on his white shirt. He would not be defeated.

"Why didn't you have the tea made sooner?" he said to me. "You see?" He pointed at them and quickly back at me, at my face. "Now they have gone away angry."

I stepped back, explaining, "The water was fresh and cold. It takes time to boil."

"You have shamed me in front of my brother. And now I am late, too." He pitched his cup down by the fire and turned and made long, angry strides toward center camp.

I leaned back against the hut doorway, ashamed now more than ever, an unserved cup of tea clenched in my hands, hot like my burning eyes.

Some long days later, while Maker was away, a group of teenage boys with muscle on their bone, appeared at our compound bearing troughs of soft mud and stacks of grass and wood, laying them like offerings on a raised spot near our circle. They had been sent by the commanders. When I saw them, I loved them like I loved my younger brothers back home, all of us still in our teens, with our dreams of marriage and children and life unfolding.

For the next few days Habsa and I cooked maize in oil for them and gave them as much clean water as we could carry. They worked before us bravely in the heat, challenging each other, laughing loudly, taking down half their work, building it back up, tearing it down again, standing the beams in different ways, sinking them deeper into mud, until finally another grass-domed hut stood humbly more or less straight up among the other thousands. But however much Habsa and I rejoiced in their work or however valiant they were in its doing, nothing could change the thing none of us suspected—that the structure was tragically doomed before it was finished. In the green wood that held up the grasses of the roof was nested a battalion of parasites.

"I'm home!" Maker returned to our compound a day after the work was complete. "I have brought another commander to see the boys' work." The man's chest was as broad as the belly of a crocodile. The creases around his eyes and in his hands held sweat and darker pigment. His breath, while he stared me up and down, came slow and rough.

"The commander and I will have some tea," my husband said. *I will make tea quicker now.* The man's eyes followed me to the cooking fire. I felt my dress melt away under his gaze and my day go dark and cold. I stiffened every muscle in my body to make my skin thick. *Turn away from me!*

"Abuk, also bring the commander some of the meat you keep." *But this small shred of goat's meat will be nothing to him.*

"I'm sorry, but there is no meat today." *God forgive me, I must save it for the small body of my boy.* "But let me put some sugar in your tea, commander."

I brought the two cups on a large flat pan, holding it carefully at each far edge, giving the commander's hand no way to brush mine. As much as Maker admired this man, I saw discomfort in his eyes too.

"Abuk, you can go to the river now to get water." Released from their service, I took a water can with one hand and Dut's hand with the other and walked away with my head up. *My arms at my sides are two walls hiding me. I will not lift the jug to my head.* I quickly put huts and people and trees and distance between me and the commander's greedy eyes.

Not long after this, my husband woke one morning saying, "What's going on?" brushing tiny specks of wood out of his hair and off his body.

"I don't know." I awoke with the same flecks in my eyes.

"I think that while we are sleeping, something has been eating our hut," Maker concluded. "Wood beetles! It must be. I will take care of it later." "Later" turned out to be never.

Soon the wood beetles hollowed out our roof beams, which then groaned under the weight of the heavy, too-green grass that crowned them.

Then Maker settled on a plan to catch the falling dust and tiny splinters. He brought home a broad, five-meter length of strong cloth, the same size used in traditional dress to wrap around the great torsos of men of power. He tied it up just below the roof, and it protected us many days from dust—but not from continuing decay.

One day an old Dinka man, winding his customary route through the camp, in his own way overseeing each person and all work, saw our hut roof tied up with a tarp. He laughed out loud and squatted down on his heels to talk to my husband.

"You better rebuild this hut entirely."

My husband, sitting stiffly against the hut's outside wall, briefly looked up, frowning. He was working intently with words on paper, framing a statement he would make when the cameras rolled in. An American news truck was on its way.

There was only a short time to prepare. He hoped this time the filmed report would get out. That this time someone would care. All this he had said to me.

But the old man insisted, "Do you want your roof to fall in on top of you?"

"Thank you, uncle. But I am busy right now. I can't do everything."

"I tell you, the next season of big rains is coming."

It was true. That morning a shadow of dark clouds slipped away with dawn, as though they'd spent the night conspiring, and then were gone.

"Do you think that tarp will save you?"

My husband scratched out words on his long yellow tablet and wrote others, frowning and rubbing his hand over the top of his head.

The old man continued, "You have to break that hut down to the ground and build a new one."

"Not now, uncle."

"You young men think you know so much. I fought in the first civil war, you know. Seventeen years. A generation lost and our fields, our villages, our families cut in pieces."

"We will not make the same mistakes your generation did."

"You already have."

"What would you have us do, uncle? We can't stop the war now that it's started."

The old man rose slowly, pulling himself up on his stick.

"Even the wildest dance will stop when the drummers stop their drumming," he said, but Maker kept his head down and his pencil on the paper. The old man continued his watchful walk.

In the heat of noon, rumors of strangers arriving at the UN Center reached our circle.

"I'll be back later." Maker left suddenly. I picked up Dut and followed at a distance. When we were close enough to see and hear, we put down out of the way, under the shade of a great tree.

Dut was soon entranced. A soft-faced white man with a bulging belly balanced a great black camera on his shoulder. The man's eyes widened as he scanned the camp's horizon from north to south, from east to west. He righted his camera often, like women do with their jugs of water, and was as gentle with it as a man is with an injured friend he carries down the road. His body and camera turned together to a distant path where two aging, weakened women walked, one leaning on the other. His eyes and the eye of his camera settled next on a motionless woman two huts away whose child was trying to wake her. He wiped the sweat out of his eyes and kept filming this way and that, stepping respectfully over stretched out legs and empty pots as he went. He seemed well accustomed to balancing on his back both the weight of his camera and the hardship of the people he filmed.

A reporter my husband's age with blue eyes and sandy hair stood dressed in khaki under the flapping blue UN flag. He spoke into the camera's square face, "In Itang, over 20 percent of the refugees are children under five. Two thirds of them arrived here suffering PEM— protein-energy malnutrition—a leading cause of death in third world children." The cameraman swiveled to his right to record a group of half-naked children gathered at this odd hour in the food distribution tent, each with yellow mash mounded on a little plate and yellow mash squeezed between their fingers and yellow mash spilling from their mouths. "This aggressive feeding plan is designed to offset malnutrition." The children were taking the mash with rare excitement, as though someone had put sugar in it today. Dut squirmed in my arms. "Not now, Dut."

Then a light-skinned man in a streaked white coat leaned into the reporter's microphone. "Our clinic has medicine but in short supply," he said. "And there is no operating theater." The cameraman swung to take a distance shot of the sturdy, concrete clinic set far off beyond the trees; he filmed the long and winding human fence of people swaying in the sun, waiting for their doctor to return.

"All these refugees came to Itang for different reasons," the blue-eyed man continued. "Achol Deng and his family came from Sudan because of local pressures and the fear of prison."

The cameraman fixed his aim on a man in a polo shirt. Fine-featured and dark-skinned, he was seated on stacked dried bricks with a blank-eyed woman, her feather-thin arm and hand resting on his thigh. With them sat a preteen girl with rows of tight braids, and behind them two half-grown boys. All fully clothed, as Christians, eyes averted from the harsh sun.

The seated man spoke to the camera, "I was arrested by government-armed local militia. They bound my hands." He held his wrists up. "I fought and escaped and fled with my family. We crossed Sudan walking to get here."

A group of grown men—Maker's co-commanders—watched the cameraman anxiously from under another tree, across the smooth courtyard from me. The blue-eyed reporter, now back in focus, continued, "Complaints have been made that relief supplies are being used by rebel troops or sold to purchase vehicles or guns. UN officials state that all such activity is strictly forbidden here. This camp is for peaceful purposes only."

A group of tall, military-age boys was gathered in the open land across from the UN building, kicking and chasing a soccer ball. The camera swung for a close-up of the group, and at one young man's command, they sat and took up sticks and hollowed wood.

The reporter went on, "Overcrowded, under supplied, the success of this camp is a credit to the Sudanese leaders. In camp on any given day you see them organizing activities, trying to make the best of things—to add some beams of hope."

My husband, a well-dressed and peaceful-looking man, stepped up to the seated boys, some of whom now raised their hollow sticks high over hollow logs while others unfolded themselves slowly to stand up. The drumbeat started low, insistent, like my heart pounds in my ears when I run. Then it stepped up to the speed of antelope in flight. The standing boys' feet now swept side to side like straw brooms clearing the rough ground; they sang out notes that reached to the tops of all the trees and to the clouds.

"Mama, it's church day!" Dut said to me.

"No, Dut, not church day."

Then the camera focused on my husband, whose eyes shifted from the camera to the commanders and back. "All of us came here because our own lands were stolen, our families killed, our future hopes crushed. By whom? The very government that promised to be at peace with us." The drummer boys kept up their beat while others leaped up in the air and played at jabbing spears. My husband smiled at their tricks. "While you are crying, you must laugh too, while you are suffering you must strengthen yourself, too, so you can help your people." His co-commanders, dressed in civilian slacks and open-collared shirts, nodded and murmured strong approval to his words, from behind the camera.

But when the cameraman turned to make an unexpected final sweep, they, like a flock of startled birds, dispersed. I also swung myself and Dut around fast, back behind the broad tree. *I can't be put on tape now, no, not in faded clothes, not with my hair undressed.* So when the probing cameraman at last stood still and lowered his camera to the dirt, there was a great relief on many sides. The boy drummers put their sticks down, the boy dancers dropped down and laid back on the ground, and my husband's colleagues regrouped, slapping congratulations on each other's backs.

"Mama, wedding day?"

"No, Dut, no, it's not wedding day."

5

A TIME TO SING

If you can walk, you can dance. If you can talk, you can sing.

I RETURNED HOME WITH THE MEMORY OF THE DARK AND FLEETING clouds of morning and the sight of more on the horizon. In fear that evening, I spoke to my husband,

"Please, let's sleep outside tonight. It will be bad if it rains and the hut falls in on you and me and Dut while we are sleeping!"

He agreed. "Tomorrow, I will have it fixed."

That night, the clouds gathered, rumbled, mounted, exploded, and spilled out months of waiting rain. Under torrents of water beating down on us, we ran from the tree back to our hut, not caring that it might collapse. By now it was just four poles sunk into the dirt, steadied by stones, with a black tarp thrown over, the grasses washed away. But our things were in there. So we stood all the rest of that night holding up the tarp with our bare hands as the water sloshed over the sides and Dut slept on a raised bed between us.

MORNING BROKE AND WITH IT MY TEMPER. AS THE RAIN STOPPED, something snapped inside me.

"You have done nothing until now to fix this, and look!" The tarp roof sagged between the poles, dipping halfway to the dirt floor, stretched past its limit like a woman's belly stretched out with child.

"Done nothing? And you? You are here all day every day." My husband pulled his shoes on. "Tell me who is doing nothing!"

"Our roof is caving in! This doesn't bother you?" Over Maker's shoulder I caught sight of two men passing by, one taller, one shorter, both silent and purposeful, walking with the same measured step.

"We can't repair it now anyway in the rains." He said. "Think about it. If we have to, we can move in with a neighbor until the weather clears."

"The neighbors are tired of us. You are a man. Think of something besides excuses!" The two men stopped a short time at a hut not far from ours. The woman in the doorway pointed toward Maker as she gathered her own children inside.

"I am certainly a man, and to me this hut is a very small matter. Why don't you fix it yourself?" He stood and straightened his shirt collar.

"Myself? How? The grasses are wet. The ground is turned to mud. There are no dry materials!"

"Now who is making excuses?" Maker picked up the men's footsteps behind him and turned on his heel.

The shorter man spoke first.

"Maker Benjamin?"

My husband squared his feet and waited. "Yes?"

"Dr. John Garang sent us to find you. He wants you to join him in Addis."

Maker did not blink. "Is there trouble?" He would follow John Garang anywhere, he respected him so much.

"No. No trouble yet."

The taller man tilted his head toward the collapsing hut and toward me, my face a crush of fear and anger. "Perhaps you need some time to take care of things before you leave?"

"No," Maker wiped the last trace of mud and wood shards from his hands. "No, she will take care of everything here."

I will take care of everything?

"Just give me time to gather my things."

He pushed past me to sort through the clothes and important papers we kept wrapped in plastic.

So this is what I get for complaining to you.

The men called over their shoulders, "Good enough, then. Find us when you're ready. We must get out of here before the rains close up the roads."

That night, Dut and I slept alone in a tent our neighbors had rigged up in case things got bad. In the days that followed, dark clouds came and went from the horizon, turning the high roads slick and weighing grasses down, making breeding grounds of standing water. Mosquitoes multiplied into hoards of winged dust.

Rain and cold wind blew through our tent, too. Though the dreaded floods never came to the camp, they did come into Dut's lungs. From the day our roof gave out, his breath became strained. A new cough, mixed with fevered restlessness, now had him burrowing underneath my arm each night to find sleep, pressing his side against mine to use the slower pace of my own breath to steady his. Even so, too often through the night we were shaken awake by his dark and bubbling cough. *Oh God, let tomorrow be a day of sun to dry his lungs.* But sun or no sun, the waters inside him would not abate. And even when the sun stayed longer in the sky, as I had begged it would, it made both grasses and mosquitoes grow, and did nothing to stop the darker growth inside Dut's lungs.

One night, as Dut lay quiet, I heard outside our tent the soft voice of an old man who lived nearby. Too old for the army, too young to die of old age, he spent his days patient and alone, watching over us from a distance.

"Abuk, good evening."

"Good evening, uncle." I rose to greet him and folded back the tent flap.

He continued, "I am sorry to trouble you, but I have come to ask for your lamp."

Ours was the only oil lamp among ten huts. A friend had given it to us for protection, and I had guarded it well.

"For you, of course." I lit its charred wick and held the lamp out for him to take.

But his arms hung at his side. There was something else.

"What is it, uncle?"

"It is just my nephew. Do not worry."

"Shall I come with you?"

"No."

"I'll come to help. Is he sick?"

"No." His hands and lips trembled.

"I'll come with you."

"All right, if you must. But leave the boy here."

Dut slept. If he woke I would hear him cough. So I turned with the old man toward his hut.

When we arrived, I raised the lamp and saw his nephew, Dao Jok, stretched out on the floor. I knew him from many days together in the camp. We all knew him. A friendly boy turned man. Now I saw his head turned flat towards the door where I entered. His forehead did not glisten with sweat, like the forehead of the sick. His open eyes did not move when I moved. There was no sound.

In the camp when bad things happened, I often heard the people weep together. But when death took this man's nephew, all was silent. There was no woman with them to make the cry. But when I raised my lamp and saw his nephew dead, I screamed. Other women woke up and came to the old man's door, lifting up their voices, too, and weeping for him and for his nephew. Habsa was there with me. Then the man's own tears could flow and life came back to him. He began to think about how to bury the young man.

In our tradition, when a young, unmarried man dies, his mother and the women of the family dress him for his burial in good clothes, in the clothes of a bridegroom. But not one woman from his family was here. His uncle did not even have a bed sheet to wrap him in.

He wept, "Do you see this? In war you lose everything. Not me, not any person in this camp, can even spare a cloth for his dead body!"

"We will sew rice bags together then." The women who had gathered spoke up. "Rice bags are white and they will cover him."

The women dispersed to gather empty sacks. When they returned, the mood was sacred as they sewed the bags together, singing softly, sewing quickly. My lamp hung in the old man's hut for them.

But I had to leave to calm myself—to see my own son's small body and to hear his breath again. The moon was higher now; there was reflected light. It lit the space inside my tent. But when I stooped to look in, Dut was on his side too; his two eyes open, reflecting light back, not blinking, like the eyes of the dead boy. *Oh, God.*

Then he whispered, "Mama, where were you?" and reached out his arms.

Men buried the old man's nephew before dawn in a shallow grave. The women wept and sang for him. I watched from the stillness of my own tent, my little boy held tight next to my heart, his breathing the only sound I really heard—shallow, labored, raspy.

"ABUK, LET'S GO!" HABSA SHOUTED IN TO WAKE ME. FIERY sunlight shot past her voice.

"Let's go. Are you still sleeping?" It was day, full day. "Gather your washing and let's go!"

"What time is it?"

"It's late. Everyone is gone already. I'm not waiting much more!"

The women used the brightest time of the day to wash. It was our best time together.

"Come on!" Habsa's arms were full of clothes. Her son, Chindut, danced and chattered at my door. Dut was up, and at the sight of the other boy came back to life.

"All right, I'm coming!" I did not remember right away what had made my sleep so heavy.

The way to the river stretched out before us like a garden in the sun. On the grasses left to right, sheets, shirts, dresses spread themselves wide open to the day—sweet, wet, clean, rippling on the sea of grass.

"You see, some have already finished!" Habsa scolded me. Women sat and gossiped all along the path as they waited for their things to dry.

"More room for us at the river then!" I said and rushed to keep up.

Every day I washed my son's clothes in boiled water by my tent. But my clothes and the clothes of my husband I washed every three days in the muddied river. Oh, my husband, now I missed him. He had made my life hard with his moods, but now I wanted him near.

"We'll have to share." Habsa turned back to let me know I had forgotten my wash tub. When the river was muddy, which was all the time, we drew the water out in tubs and waited to let the silt settle. There were few latrines, and the people relieved themselves along the shore. In the rainy season it all washed down. Only lye soap and the science of tubs could save us.

"Habsa, you go first." I skimmed bowl after bowl of water off the river's top and poured it out to fill her tub. We waited for the dark brown water to clear.

Other women were still at their washing there, too. Song filled the air.

Ay ya, ay ya ya.
Sons of Southern Sudan
Are never scared to fight.
Yes, yes, we are men.
Even if we die our country wins.
Ay ya, ay ya ya.
Yes, yes, we are women.
Even if we die our country wins.

"Who made this song?" I asked. "That person was never in this camp! No one who has lived here will ever sing about war again!"

"Just sing it and don't think so much," a woman laughed. "Just sing. It will make you feel strong."

Ay ya, ay ya ya.
Yes, yes, we are women.
Even if we die our country wins.

They sang songs of weddings, too. A tall lady from Habsa's hometown was feeling good and opened her mouth to sing,

I am going to have a wedding,
Yes, I'm going to get married,
Just so I can invite my friends!

Everybody laughed, and she made a big circle with her arm.

I'll invite Habsa, the smiling one!

Habsa shook her head.

I'll invite Abuk, the quiet one!

I turned away, laughing.

I'll invite Christine, the lazy one!

Christine stood up and threw her soap in the water.

"I'm not the lazy one!"

"Then you're not invited!"

Yes, I'm going to get married,
Just so I can invite my friends!

A woman with five or six years more than me kept silent during the song, just washing, washing, rubbing soap across the same place again and again. I went close and spoke to her,

"Sister, how are you?" Dut followed me.

"Is he your boy?" she asked, drying her hands.

"Yes, he is."

"How old?" She held her hands out and took his hands.

"Three."

"My boy was three, too." Dut tried to pull away. She held him.

"Where is your boy now?" I asked.

She looked down and slowly picked up her wash again. "You have to do everything to keep your child alive, because in the camp if you lose your child, it is something that will never go out of your mind."

Now that she had let go of him, Dut sat down quietly beside her.

She went on, "It is one thing to lose a child knowing that you have given him the best. You will not feel guilty then."

He splashed his hands in the water of her tub and popped her used-up bar of soap out through his fingers.

"But in this place, in this terrible place, you really blame yourself.

Did I give my child the best? No! I gave my child the worst possible life!"

Dut dribbled water on her arms and painted her face with it until you could not tell her tears from the river water.

"God knows," I told her. But I didn't know if He knew at all.

I learned over time that clothes washed in this river slowly changed their color. I had a pink patterned silk dress and a flowered one of blue. They soon became dull and drab as the sand. In fact, you could tell how long a person had been here by the color of their clothes. But to tell the truth, I always saw my favorite bright blue dress as blue; in my eyes it faded, but in my mind it never did.

"Abuk, are you finished now? Let's go." The sun had moved across the sky, and Habsa's son was crying for food. The women's songs and laughter had long ago taken wing.

"The clothes are dry enough," I said, and gathered them and turned myself and Dut to walk with Habsa and her son back home.

I CAN'T TELL YOU WHEN THIS NEXT EVENT HAPPENED BECAUSE THIS night stands alone in my mind's eye, disconnected from anything before or after. In the middle of this night, Dut woke up to a brutal fit of coughing.

Maybe the medicines the UN hospital gave me were just wrong. Maybe they were too old or weakened by the sun.

But this night, while I held Dut close, I felt heat filling up his body, his rib cage ballooned, tight with the work of each breath. His muscles pulled hard, but less and less breath came.

I had to get him to the hospital.

But that was not going to be easy. All day, thick clouds had covered us and now this night there was no moon or stars. The tent was not as safe as the hut had been. The tarp did not reach to the ground on any side, so any animal that wanted to could crawl in during the night—snakes, rats, or other hungry things. Though we were somewhat safe on our wooden bed frame, whenever I stepped down after dark, I prayed, "Oh God, protect me." For emergencies I kept two batteries, carefully put by like two gold bars, for a flashlight that I'd found. Whenever I got out of bed in the dark, I went with fear, the flashlight in my hand.

But now, Dut suddenly leaned into me and began to turn his head left and right, left and right. I felt the hollow underneath his breast-bone deepen. The air in his lungs screeched like the cry of vultures. Then the sound stopped. He struggled and went still.

That instant, I jumped up and ran. My feet, not my eyes, found the path outside as I pounded Dut's back over and over until again he gasped for air.

On a good day it was at least a half hour walk on the main road. Cutting straight across through the bush was the quicker way tonight. I plunged in and felt a foot-worn path under me. But all sight was gone.

"My flashlight! I left it!" But I had no way to go back for it. People thought at times they had heard lions in the bush, and I had often felt the growl of hyena close by the camp. At night they came near to look for flesh. So now I held Dut to my chest to muffle his gasps and slowed my pace a while to dull the noise of my own steps.

"My God, just let us live. Just let me and my son live."

Even if the lions or hyena did not hear us, they might catch our scent. It all depended on the turning of the wind. "Oh, God, help us." If there were snakes on the path, I would have to let them bite. Between the gasps of Dut's breath, I heard the chattering of my own teeth.

Then the path cleared. Lights flickered behind gray windows. Soon I was in the glare of the hospital hallway, my son's mouth stretched out like the mouth of a fish, his shoulders pulled up to suck in the least bit of air. The night attendant ran to wake the doctor.

After the injection, the doctor rebuked me.

"Woman, why did you wait until now? Your boy almost died!"

He sat down hard on the metal chair against the wall and kept his eyes on both of us until our breathing slowed to normal. Things were calmer now. Dut climbed into the doctor's lap and talked into his stethoscope, and then we laughed together with the simple joy of still being foolishly alive.

"Achol, make them a place," he said to the attendant. "They'll stay here until morning."

In the shadows of the back hall I cradled Dut until dawn. I had my own quiet song.

Mother, I am writing you a long letter
I have so much to tell.
Mother, I am singing you this long letter
Because my heart needs you to know.

6

LEARNING TO STAND

The past is in your head, but the future is in your hand.

IT WAS TIME TO FIX A BETTER LIFE FOR MY SON. I COULD NOT KEEP him alive under a tarp draped over poles. I could not sleep forever in the hospital. The next morning I left Dut with Habsa and went to find a man by the name of Tong Ajak, who was well known for the strength of the wood he used for building, known to all as a good and honest man.

I found him near the edge of camp. "Uncle Ajak, I need your help to build a new hut."

"Do you have money to buy the wood and grass?"

"I have fifty *birr*."

"It is enough. I will gather ten men and bring your wood from the forest."

"Uncle, I must come with you. I must see the wood when they cut it, that it is strong and has no beetles."

"You will not come. In the bush there are lions and hyena. I take people who have spears or guns. You have neither. Stay in the camp with your child."

I knew about these dangers. I also had heard stories of men, both Nuer and Dinka, hiding in the bush to kill each other. Our tribes had always been at war. Even here in the camp, where we were all just trying to survive, even now, you would hear about a Dinka man being killed by Nuer tribesmen, or a Nuer man found dead in the forest, murdered. Tong Ajak and I were Dinka. We knew such men were more dangerous than lions. But I also knew Tong Ajak was tough and brave. I knew that if there was an attack, he would not run.

I insisted.

He fixed his eyes on the forest, straining to see into it and to see into the future.

"We go and come out quickly. We go with ten men so we can work fast and leave." He turned to me, "Tomorrow, early morning. You will bring water for us all. We'll meet here. Can you do it?"

"I will do it, uncle. Thank you." *I will not sleep tonight.*

I made many water-carrying trips, first at night from the river to my hut to boil and strain it, and then in the morning back to the edge of the forest. Carrying the heavy pots on my head, as women do, hurt my neck badly. Then when Ajak told me they would do the building, too, I realized I would be serving them every day till they finished. My neck hurt worse thinking about it.

Tong Ajak arrived early with me. When the last worker finally arrived, we set out.

We entered the bush on foot by a narrow, uneven road, walking one after the other in a single line. The men carried the water and the tools. I carried an axe. The men sang in loud voices to drive off animals. We were tense and watchful.

Tong Ajak led us to a place with good wood. We pushed ourselves to work fast. First, a man would cut a tree down, then others would leap on it and cut it into lengths, then others quickly bound the lengths with cords. I helped the binders, pulling and rolling felled trees into bundles. After each task we would stop dead still, ears cocked. The men worked with spears laid near them on the ground. Tong Ajak kept watch with a gun.

When the wood was enough, Ajak ordered us to stop. At his word, we again formed a single line and began the heavy walk home, hauling water pots and staggering under loads of lumber.

Blisters formed on my hands, opened up, bled. My feet were

swollen into the shape of men's feet. But we were alive and we had wood; good, solid wood.

They told me it would take seven days to build the hut.

Every night I made many trips to the river, then worked to boil and strain the water so it would be cool to drink the next morning. For something as simple as drinking cool water, you had to plan and work and wait.

I also cooked them three meals a day. In seven days, I cooked my whole month's ration of maize, beans, oil, and salt from the UN.

It is not simple to build a strong hut. Every piece has a measure. Every piece has a place. First you dig a broad hole into the ground and stand wood posts up inside, the structure. Then you circle them with stacked wood, laid flat like the horizon, and tie the slats fast to the posts. Once the wooden walls are set, you must plaster them with thick mud inside and out. Then the grass for the roof must be woven. Each part is made to fit into the next, and all parts must be joined and double-joined. This is not something you can do while you are fighting.

Though the men rested at night those seven days, I could not. My eyes would not easily close. I was remembering my mother and father and brothers and sisters back home in Sudan. I regretted leaving them for my husband. And now he might never return. Building this hut was taking all our money and all our food. After finishing this hut, my son and I might go hungry inside it.

So, while I couldn't sleep, I prayed, "God help us, just let my son and me live." There was always more that I wanted to say, but I could only get these few words out again and again, "God help us, just let my son and me live," until I fell asleep or until the sun rose and it was time for my body to stand up again.

On the seventh day, my hut was finished. The men gathered up their tools and left. But I kept working.

When hut walls dry, they're like concrete. I polished mine inside and out. I was able to make them shine because I used mud from a special place, away from the latrines and other huts. You can't buy this kind of mud, but people show you where to find it. And then later when you see a crack in your wall, you go get more of the same and polish your walls again, if you are still strong enough.

The good huts last for two or three years if you keep them repaired and don't fall sick at the time that something goes wrong. But in the flood season, the UN cannot get food to you. So you might go a long time without eating and become too weak to polish or rebuild. Then water, snakes, or rats come in, and you become a sick, starving person inside a ruined hut. I did not want to let that happen to me and my son.

IN THE NEXT RAINY SEASON, ALL AROUND THE PLACE MY HUT WAS SET was deep mud and standing water mixed with diseases and with death. It was standing between my hut and the others in our circle, sending up a foul smell. So when people would come across the way to see me, their feet would be full of that kind of foul water. And when I went to see them, my feet were the same. So I looked for an extra *tishet*, as we call it, a round tub that we used to wash clothes, and I put it in front of my hut door and kept it filled with clean water. I love my Sudanese people and I would never refuse to welcome them in. But the place inside was also for my son. So that tub of water was my welcome mat and the only way into my new home.

Not many days after this, the hunger I'd feared came to my door. I had been many long months in the camp. Maker had been gone during the most difficult times. I had been fighting my depression by building and holding on for the next month's rations. I had been putting off my son's hunger by counting out only a little bit of food each day. In the morning of this day, I cooked our last grains of rice and mixed them with the last drops of bean milk. Now, our pot was completely empty. In truth, there was not a grain of rice anywhere anymore. The UN had not been able to get food to the camp for a very long time because of the rains. My neighbors and I had also withdrawn from one another from the shame of having nothing to share.

Three days of no food passed; only tears filled my stomach. It was late now, and I sat with my son, just staring at the sun's setting, seeing a horizon full of days just like this one, coming like soldiers to end our lives. Now every day I was just sitting, not knowing what to do after this. So this day I did not light the evening fire for cooking because there was to be no more food. I just sat and prayed, "Oh God, help me. Show me what to do."

Then Mama Ager Goom, the first woman to take arms in Anyanya One, passed by to greet and to bless me. But when she saw me sitting like that, she got mad.

"Why are you sitting like this with no fire?"

I knew it was wrong to sit at the time of meals without a fire burning. In our tradition, even if you have nothing to eat you must do something so that others will think you have food. But that day everything was gone and I had lost all my hope.

"You must light the fire," she said. "Then you will have something."

I felt ashamed she had found me like this. She took Dut up in her arms and spoke to him softly while I lit the fire. Then she took out fifty *birr*.

"Abuk, have these," she said. "I have sold my good watch."

"Mama Ager, I cannot take this from you. You will need it for your own family."

"I have something else I can sell, Abuk. Take this money now."

I knew that I should not resist her. The next day I would go outside the camp and buy from the Ethiopians. My son and I would have something to eat and something to share with the others. I added more wood to the fire so that everyone in the circle could see it.

"Thank you, thank you," I kept saying.

But that night, my thoughts turned to how she had gotten the money. I remembered the first week of camp, how I had told the others I would not sell my things because Maker would take us to a better place. Now I could see things more clearly.

Even so, I did not like what I had to do. Many times since Maker had left, I had taken out the pretty things I brought with me, to touch them and feel again what living a good life was like. In those

moments I could stop feeling like a lost person because I held in my
hands the proof of the better world that I belonged to. To me those
pretty things were like a friend's arm that a drowning person holds
onto in deep water. But now I must let them go and learn to swim.

The money from Mama Ager was soon gone and we were
without food again. I began choosing which dresses I would sell. I
had twelve with me. One dress was the color of the sky, with
flowers the color of champagne, made of a polished cloth that shim-
mered in the sun. It was from England, a gift from my sister-in-law.
I had worn it to my wedding reception dinner. Whenever I touched
that one, bright memories of my family's wedding party filled my
eyes.

I decided to keep that one back. No, I would not sell that one. I
would sell the others first. That would be enough. My dresses were
beautiful. The Ethiopians would love them. If I could get at least
eighty *birr* for each dress and if I sold eleven, we could buy two small
bottles of milk each day for at least twelve months before I would
have to let the best one go. *If it goes this way, it will not be so bad. In
a year, surely, we will go back to Sudan.*

That night, I found a few tea leaves to boil for Nijiang and the
next morning woke early to ask for her help. We had not had morning
tea together since the rainy season.

"Auntie Nyjang, please come take tea with me this morning," I
told her. She came, and I asked if she would go outside the camp with
me to help me sell some of my clothes. She agreed, pleased to see I
had come to my senses.

The Ethiopians lived north of the camp. The path was long. Back
when I had money, I would walk it every day, very early, bringing
two *birr* and two empty bottles in my hand for milk.

This was a small village made of only twenty families, but its
population was growing. Each day more lost boys arrived as refugees
and stayed there outside the camp. Today, we arrived late in the morning. Some Ethiopian women were cooking outside; others were
spreading clothes out to dry. Their light brown skin and long black
hair distinguished them. Flies were everywhere because their goats
and sheep lived with them and because of the way they killed them

for food. But the village did not have the bad smell of the camp. It even had a concession stand with soda and beer.

Nyjang took me first to a large hut, owned by a man who before the rainy season had traded much with the Itang refugees. We found him standing out back with a bloody machete in his hand. A small goat hung by its feet before him, blood still draining from its neck. He looked our way when Nyjang and I stopped in front of his place.

"Peace to you," said Nijang. We shared the Arabic language with these neighbors.

"Peace to *you,*" the man answered, lowering his machete.

"Sir, we have some things to sell. Can you buy?"

"Not now, woman. I am busy with my own things. But when you have sold your goods, come back here and buy meat from me." He turned back to the hanging goat and brushed away the gathering flies. Soon he would be building a fire to burn off its hair.

We walked on to the hut of an old Nuer woman who lived among them and owned a cow. She was boiling some milk for herself and for her grandchildren playing raucously nearby.

"Greetings, Maleh!" Nyjang called to her. "It has been a long time since I have seen you! How are you?"

"How are you, Nyjang? What is it I can do for you?" She pointed to a second pot waiting by the fire. "See? I still have some milk from this morning that you can buy if you like."

"We have come first to sell some of Abuk's things. Would you like to look at a dress? Very pretty." As she was saying this, I extended my right arm to show the two beautiful dresses I had brought with me.

She turned her face to Nyjang. "I cannot look at these now. I am boiling milk and then I will prepare some for you to buy. Leave your bottles here. I will fill them."

"We cannot. We have no money yet. We need to sell Abuk's things first."

"God help you, then," she said, and turned back to her boiling pot.

The sun was higher in the sky now, and the heat was beginning to press in on me. I thought of Dut waiting for me to return with something he could eat.

"Abuk, let's go to the hut of Mulu. She trades in Gambela. If she has cash she can buy your dresses here and sell them there for more."

This woman lived in the western part of the village. Even from a distance, you could tell hers was the hut of a trading woman. Broad redstone steps led up to it, with red, white, and yellow flowers blossoming on each side. Clay bowls painted with black and brown designs and an array of pretty plastic shoes of every color were arranged in the shade under her front roof. Some potatoes lay next to them. We approached her door.

"Mulu? Are you in there?"

"Is that Nyjang?" She came out into the sunlight, a woman older than Nyjang, with some of her side teeth missing. Her skin, lighter than ours, was lined and spotted from the sun. "What would you like to buy this morning? It has been too long since I have seen you." She squeezed tobacco juice out between her teeth and spit it into the dirt.

"Anchee Mulu, it is we who have come to sell to you. Abuk has brought two pretty dresses to show you."

"I do not have cash to spend right now. Since the rains, trading has almost stopped. People cannot travel. I am just struggling to keep myself alive." She squinted. "But tell me, what do you have to sell?"

I took the two dresses from my arm and laid them out on the large mat that was spread out near her cooking fire. They were beautiful in the sun, the flower patterns as bright as the first day I bought them. She examined them a long time.

"I can give you 10 *birr* for one and no more."

"Only 10 *birr*? That is only five days of milk!"

Her expression did not change. I tried to quickly recalculate everything. *Then every few days I will have to sell a dress. In a few weeks they will all be gone and we will still have nothing! No, that can't happen!*

I hoped that perhaps she did not understand. I spoke to her again, "Look at this dress more closely, feel it. This dress is from England. By itself it cost one hundred times what you have offered and it is still new!"

"I cannot give you what I do not have."

I looked at Nyjang. "Thank you, but I don't think I can sell these right now." I gathered the dresses up quickly and got up to go.

Nyjang stood in my way. "Abuk, you cannot go home today with nothing. Your money is gone. None of us has anything. The UN's food is not getting through yet. And even if it did, you know your son cannot keep that food long in his stomach. You have to do this."

My throat was getting tight. Where was my husband? Why had I not heard from him?

With Nyjang's eyes on me, I kneeled back down and slowly spread out my dresses again. I pulled my hands back. "Here you are. Take whichever you would like. Ten *birr* is fine."

When we got back to camp with enough coins for only a few days' milk, my head and my fists were pounding.

MY SON HAD NOT BEEN HEALTHY. I KNEW IT WAS THE SICKNESS IN the air, the damp, the little food. The only thing I could do was to make the space inside our hut different from the camp. I kept it dry and polished for him.

It was late afternoon, when I was just putting Dut down to sleep, that I heard a low, male voice at my door. I did not recognize it.

"Hello? Hello...is someone in there?" I looked up and saw a stranger near the doorway, outlined against the evening sun, standing with his feet apart. He looked fit, muscular, maybe twenty, twenty-one years old, like me. Why is he looking in here? I turned back to Dut, to cover him for the night.

"Abuk? I'm looking for Abuk Makuac."

I didn't want him to wake up my son, so I got up and went to the door to answer him. He raised his hand and backed away. "Who are you?" I asked.

When he opened his mouth to answer, coughing overcame him. He couldn't stop it, and was soon doubled over, his back toward me, tight like a fist, fingers digging into his knees. Between fits, he would steady himself and slowly suck in air.

I waited while he got control. Then I stepped closer and spoke to him.

"Please, what can I do for you?"

"This cough...," he paused, and while his mind was focused on breathing in, I looked at him more closely. His pants were torn but had been part of a uniform. He had no belt, no shirt. But strength showed in his arms. Now he was looking at me.

"Are you Abuk?"

"Yes, I am."

"I am Monydit...your cousin." He stopped to draw breath again and wait for more strength. Whenever he fell to coughing, he became someone weak, very weak. "I am back...from the fighting."

He was still leaning forward. "I'm sorry. This cough...has made...me useless."

I could hear air whistling through his lungs.

"I need a place...to stay to get well.... No one will take me in...like this.... Your husband told me...I can stay here." He straightened up a little and leaned against the wall of the hut. "But if it does not please you...to keep me...I will go to the center."

So, he was my cousin. This soldier who could not breathe was family. In our Sudanese tradition, you do not chase away any family member. You take him in, even if you have never seen him before, even if he is sick.

What about my baby sleeping inside? So small and sick now too. My mind was turning but to hesitate long in answering a plea for help was a very bad thing. I was wrong to be taking so long.

So I told him, "You are welcome to stay here."

Sweat was beaded up on his face. When I welcomed him, he wiped it from around his eyes and nodded to me. But he was holding himself back from speaking. He asked with signs if he could go off for a short time and come back. I let him know I would wait.

It was only after he left that I looked at the ground where he had been bent over coughing. There in the dirt, mixed with his spit, I saw bright red blood. "Oh, God," I said. I went in quickly to prepare a place for him in the farthest corner of the hut, away from where Dut was sleeping. "God, help us."

He does not force himself on us. I will let him sleep far from us in that corner. I will feed him maize and water. I will get him well before his sickness can pass to my son.

Over time, it turned out to be a good thing to have him with us. Dut grew to like him, and finally we were not alone. In the days to come he regained his strength and, as long as he stayed, shared it generously.

TIME BREAKS DOWN

When vultures surround you, try not to die.

YOU MUST UNDERSTAND, MY MEMORIES OF THE CAMP COME IN fragments. Everyone lost track of days and times there. My memory has no way to organize the happening of things, so the scenes I remember lie scattered everywhere like torn books on a dusty floor. But I will open them to you as they come.

One evening after eating, I fell into a hard sleep before I had washed my hands. I always washed my hands and Dut's hands with soap—but this night, no. I was too tired. In the middle of the night—I don't know when it was; the moon was high and the camp silent except for the call of hyena in the bush—I was dreaming and waking and dreaming. Then a sharp pain jolted me out of my sleep—shooting up from my hand through my arm like lightning. I looked down and in the moonlight I saw a rat hanging from my hand, his teeth sunk into it, still biting, trying to take a piece of my flesh. I sat up and screamed and banged my hand against the wall until he went limp. I heard his body hit the floor.

I grabbed the flashlight and in two steps I was across the room to check Dut. I squeezed the blood out of my own thumb and washed it over and over with water from the big pot. I knelt there trembling for the longest time, shining the flashlight this way and that. I searched the length of Dut's body and the cloth where he lay and the corner where Monydit now lay coughing and turning.

I had been careless. But the rat came to me first and not Dut. I did not fall sick from it. God helped us, and I learned from this never to fall asleep again without washing. After that too I always kept the flashlight very close to me. And almost always it had batteries inside.

It was the hottest part of the day in the camp—a neighbor came running to my hut.

"Abuk, Ajwong's first wife has left him." Her voice had fear in it. "There was a fight. She just got up and left. It happened this morning, now no one can find her."

In the camp, sometimes on a bad day people would kill themselves. And it would start this way. At first you couldn't find them. And then when you found them they were dead, killed by their own hand, or by lion or by heat.

I asked Habsa to come with me quickly and look for her. Our eyes swept through the walkways of the camp as we ran from hut to hut. She was nowhere. Then we spotted her young son standing alone behind a hut, weeping, his face toward the camp's far western boundary.

"Where is your mother?"

He would not look at us.

He kept his eyes fixed on the forest. We were more afraid then.

Habsa and I continued in the direction of his gaze. Along the way we called her name, asked people if they had seen her. Some had, some had not. Those who had saw her going that way much earlier, in the morning.

We walked faster and called louder. Then we found her at the edge of the bush, sitting under a tree. Just sitting and scratching the ground. Her eyes staring ahead like her son's, seeing nothing.

I knelt down and asked her, "Auntie Nyjang, what are you doing here?"

She scratched the ground in silence.

I asked her again, "Why did you come here?"

She looked ahead, breathing deeper, letting words come back to her throat, "I had to leave my hut. My husband."

Her face was swollen, with fist marks darkening. But there was no emotion, no life in her. She meant to stay under this tree until she died.

I told her, "You'd better go home."

Her vacant eyes asked me why.

"Because you have nowhere to go, because none of us have anywhere to go."

The sun was too hot. We knelt down with her under that big tree. Sweat poured down my back. "If you've got a problem with your husband, you have to solve it. Both of you have to solve it. Sitting here will not help you. Something may happen. An animal could come and eat you."

She was not moving at all, not even brushing the flies from her face. "Just go back," I said. "Go home and ignore everything. You are not happy. None of us are happy. We are all angry."

My knees were aching. But I stayed down. Then I put my two hands on her shoulders and told her, "Habsa and I need you with us."

A frown came over her face as her eyes turned to focus on us and on the things around her.

"Auntie Nyjang, please come back with us."

She looked at me and at my friend and at the forest. We respected her with our silence.

After a long wait, she pulled herself to her feet and said, "Please come with me. I'm going home to watch my child."

We went back with her to her hut. When we got there her son and husband were outside. Her husband did not look up or speak. She took her boy, went inside, and set to cooking.

I knew her husband would not say a word to her or to us, that he would hold his peace. I knew this because he needed her. In this place sometimes the only peace we could keep was our silence. And that was good enough.

IT MIGHT HAVE BEEN DURING THE SECOND YEAR I WAS THERE. IT HAD been a long time since a food truck had arrived at the distribution tent. It had been a long while since we had come out of our huts to greet each other in the morning with tea and had food to share.

I always found food for Dut. My saved food was for him, not for me. But the hunger was wearing on me. When my strength dissolved, thoughts and memories swirled together like lumps of cornmeal and water in my mind. I couldn't feel my mind right.

It happened late one day, when the sun reflected off my empty tin cup. It glittered in my eyes the way light used to glitter off of the silver tray I carried to guests in my father's house. Oh, that tray was beautiful and full, with soft, flat *kisra* bread on the flowered plate, and beef and sautéed onion stew in the great bowl. On the side, in the crystal bowl, tomato sliced into onion, oil and leafy green *jir jir*, fresh from our garden. Water with lemon and sugar before the meal. Sweet tea afterwards.

I brought all of these things to our guests on the great, sparkling silver tray. Their eyes and smiles would grow bigger with each pass.

"Abuk," Habsa called out in the circle's silence. "Come look, down the road. New people are coming."

Guests! The table is spread. I stood to join her, but was still in my dream.

"Look, they have come a long way."

In front, a young man, bone thin, silent. Two women, behind. A teenage boy next, in his arms a small girl child with shoulders like the wings of a tiny bird. They walked together but did not have the look of family—except for the same cracked lips and the same failing pulse of a slow, slow march toward camp.

In my father's house when guests arrived, we gave them one of our own rooms for as long as they wanted. When they came, they were the center of our attention, the treasured vessel into which we poured all our best.

"What can we give them?" Habsa asked me.

"I don't know," I answered. "They look hungry, Habsa. I will make *kisra* and stew, and hot flat beans. And you bring cold cheese and milk."

"Abuk, what's wrong with you?"

I looked around for my silver tray.

"Abuk, when you don't eat, you become foolish." She grabbed my arm. "Come with me. I have a little cornmeal. You will eat something right now."

"But Dut?" *Where is my silver tray?*

"You fed him this morning. We must take these people to the registration tent and hope there will be rations for them there."

In the distance more travelers drew near. After eating a little with Habsa, my eyes could see things as they were again.

As far as I could see down the road, scattered bundles of stick figures tall and short, straight and stooped, were coming, some dragging things, some holding onto each other. People usually came a few families at a time, but this day it looked like hundreds. We met some while they were on the way in.

A young man spoke for them. "Where are we?"

"This is Itang camp."

"What kind of camp is it?"

"It is a UN camp."

"Thank God," he said. "We will be alright now. We will be alright now." The others behind him said, "Thank God," and those behind them said the same. As word spread down the road, thanks and tears spread too.

THE CAMP BEGAN TO STIR, TOO, WITH THE NEWS OF THEIR ARRIVAL. Women gathered cups for water. They up-ended empty pots and bowls in hope of finding more scraps of food to share.

"Where have you come from?"

"We have crossed the river. We have come from Bahr al Ghazal."

"Is this all of you?"

"There were hundreds when we set out. But not now."

"How far have you walked?"

"Three months' journey. Snakes and lion got some on the way, and thirst, and drowning, and sometimes the enemy, and sometimes the civil war defectors."

More people from the camp were coming out as word spread that there were arrivals. I stayed by a small boy, about seven, who ran to me at first sight. I invited him and his little sister to the shade of my tree and sat down with them. My heart was beating very hard, and I was dizzy from the effort.

"Where is your mother?" I asked the boy.

He hugged me. And for many days after that the boy wouldn't leave my side.

I must offer these people a place to sleep. I must give them food. Where is my silver tray? Tears came up in my eyes. That's when Dut, who had been wandering, found me and lay down beside me too.

Habsa knew I wasn't myself again and said, "Abuk, it's alright. Stay here. I will take them to registration."

But some new arrivals were already collapsing—from both exhaustion and relief. Their surrendered bodies lay strewn throughout the entrance to the camp. There were dozens of people from the camp around me now, shouting this way and that.

"Go to the UN Center! Tell them!"

"Bring pots with water!"

"Find corn to boil! Find corn! There's nothing to give them!"

I felt the force of people pounding past me, the urgency of voices, as I lay back against my tree, my eyes closed, to calm my dizzy mind, my own barely assuaged hunger. The little boy and his sister, now lay still and close to me. Their innocence slipped into me, and my mind played tricks. I was three years old again....

"Abuk! Abuk! Take Juma's hand!" My mother is shouting and shouting. Her eyes open wide like her mouth and her hands. "Juma! Juma! Take Abuk's hand!" My little heart stands up. And Mama and Juma and I run with the whole town. Juma swings me up onto his hip because my legs are too short to keep up.

I love Juma. He is fourteen and he is strong. His parents died in a raid in the spring, so he is my brother now.

Juma runs with me on his back. I am safe. I hear loud popping above the splashing of the rain. Banging like when corn pops in a pan. We run through stinging, screaming things. I bury my face in Juma's neck and feel his heartbeat and feel the rain hit our faces and the high grass whip our legs.

I look back and see many soldiers pointing long guns. My aunties and uncles and cousins and friends are running too. Some fall. I hold on tight to Juma's neck as we bounce up and down on his running feet.

Then more pops and Juma falls and our faces crash and slide through the stems of the tall grass. His eyes close." Juma! Juma! Wake up, Juma!" He won't move. A hand grabs my arm and pulls me through the wet grass. "Juma's hurt! Juma's hurt!" I yell at them and stretch my neck to see behind us. Someone stops and kneels down where he fell.

The boy I'd taken home was still under the tree with me, curled up asleep, but his legs were pumping lightly, as if in a dream. His little sister was asleep now too, quiet in my arms.

A larger group of refugees was coming down the road now. Right away, more women from the camp went out to meet them. "Maybe my brother, my husband, my sister, maybe my mother are among these new arrivals," they cried as they ran. And their hopes gave them strength to run all the way down the road to meet them.

"Abuk, if the children are sleeping now, please come and help us." *I want to help, but my mind is crying, "Juma! Juma!"*

"All right, Habsa," I said, "All right, I am coming." But I was not happy to leave Juma like that in my memories, nor leave the boy sleeping who reminded me of him. *I have to keep remembering. I have to keep feeling it to the end, when my mother and I and Juma are together again, in an empty hut by the trees and I'm stroking his hair and she's washing his wound.*

In those days, when my todays and yesterdays mixed together like mash to feed my fading mind, I often got lost. *Where am I? Who am I?* And in those times of hunger few had the strength to help me find my way back. But Dut knew me well; when to ask for things and when to let me be.

"Abuk, you can carry this big jar. I have another." Habsa's voice was loud and full of excitement. She was having a hard time slowing down enough to walk next to me. I could feel her feet wanting to catch up with her eyes and get to the river and back before more new people came. The last time she was like this was that first day, when we discovered each other here in the same camp.

"Abuk, you know I already talked with some of the ones that got here first! I gave a dress to that one woman...."

I was still feeling weak, and my belly was hurting even from carrying an empty jar. I tried to take my mind off the pain by watching the men working by the banks of the river ahead. It looked like they were digging.

"That woman is just happy to be here now and she told me her story, and we were just laughing...."

All I had to do was keep walking next to Habsa, because when she was happy, she didn't need anybody to encourage her to talk.

"Abuk, when the soldiers attacked her village, no one had any time to take anything. Everyone just ran to the bush and hid there. All night and all the next day they hid there because the soldiers that attacked her village were still around, looking for more cattle and more people. The next night she and her neighbors decided they had to leave the forest and run away from their village forever. But the soldiers heard them and chased them down. They grabbed this woman's clothes right off her back as she ran—but she got away!"

We were getting closer to the river. I could see that the men were digging some kind of channel, maybe for more latrines, or to drain the water from the campground.

"When morning came, there she was—running naked! Ooooh, she was so ashamed and nobody had even one piece of cloth to give her to cover herself!"

"So what did she do?" Now I was listening and curious.

"Eventually on the road she passed a lady who told her, "I can give you this rice sack if you want to cover up." So my friend sat down right then and there and sewed that sack into a skirt and sewed a piece of wire into it, to tie it onto her."

The men were picking things up out of the ground and tossing them away from the bank. Light, round objects and what looked like long clubs and pieces of cloth.

"But she says she was a little bit fat and the skirt came up really short, so the kids running away with her just really laughed!" Habsa giggled and wanted to catch my eye but that was the moment when I made out just exactly what the men were digging up: The round things were human skulls! The clubs were leg and arm bones. Now the men were taking them up bone by bone, clearing the way to make a canal.

Habsa continued, "Today when she put on one of my UN dresses, she held her old rice sack skirt up to herself, turning like she was modeling for a movie. We were laughing!"

I wondered, *Is it a good idea for those men to disturb the dead?*

"She says she's going to save that skirt and when she gets out of here and has a family, she will show it off to her children!"

Where will I be buried? I wondered. As we drew nearer and nearer to the river, I kept Habsa between myself and the men. She was too excited to stop talking. I was too upset to keep listening.

Little by little my hope had been dropping. I had been waiting for my husband to call for me. But by now that was just a dream. And since the beginning I could not renew myself at all with sleep. Sad thoughts would not leave my mind night or day. And now this tearing pain inside my belly. I had begun to envy the dead who, without pain, without fear, without hunger, without thirst, lie peacefully. But now, seeing these men digging through their graves and tossing their bones aside, I was afraid I would not find rest in death either.

"Abuk, look there! The people have already met more on the road! They're already welcoming them!" She wanted to run to join in, so I turned to follow, swinging the water jug up to carry it on my head. Then I felt a sharp pain between my eyes and down my spine.

"Habsa, help me!" My neck could not take the weight of a full jug today. Habsa put her jug down quickly to help me with both hands.

"Abuk, it's alright. Just bring it down slowly. Here, let it rest on your shoulder." She was right. The pain was less with the jug resting there. She swung down to pick up her own jug again. "All right, let's get going!" When Habsa was happy, she couldn't feel sorry for anyone. But she did slow down her pace a little and started to walk behind me, just to keep her eye on both me and the water jug.

I walked back slowly, balancing the jug on my shoulder. Left foot, right foot. Left foot, right foot. Without looking back again at the river, without thinking again about the dead, until we got back to the camp.

Little children ran behind their mothers out of the camp toward the road. Many people from the camp were out there already, greeting the new arrivals, arms stretched out, welcoming them, holding them up, walking them in. The camp people and the new arrivals, two groups walking together on the same road. Which group was happier, I could not tell. Which group had more tears, I could not tell.

Habsa and I put down our water near the cooking circle, where some were already boiling the grains of corn and preparing the drinking water these arriving ones would need.

Then Habsa and I walked out to them too. Seeing gratitude fill the cracks in their faces, my heart revived a bit too. But how weak and how thin and how ill they were, and how few small children and how few elderly were among them!

"Welcome to you! How are you? How are you?" We started calling.

"Where are you from? How are you doing?"

Over and over again, we just kept holding this one and then that one and asking, "How are you? How are you?"

Then I heard a shriek from Habsa, "Auntie Alual, it is you!"

It was Auntie Alual, from Habsa's family, and behind her a woman who was a friend of my mother.

"Auntie Ageir, is it you?" I called to her. "How are you?"

"Abuk, is it you? You are so skinny I didn't know you!"

"Auntie, how are you? Have you heard, where is my mother?"

"Abuk, she is all right. I have heard she is in Wau still. But I also heard she is worried about you!"

We walked with these two into the camp, our arms around them, our questions welcoming them. The bright joy of this moment burned through the fog in my mind. I could think now, and my stomach could rest.

Three or four teenage boys were following us, too. Their legs like broken tree branches. Their skin was baked like the back of crocodiles. But, oh, they were happy. Their smiles were from one ear to the other and they were hanging on us and talking to us like we were their mothers and sisters.

Like us, other people of the camp brought back from the road groups of people like these. Habsa and I brought ours to our circle of huts and sat them down and gave them clean water, a little at a time, to drink.

"I'm so happy to lie down here!" one boy said.

"The lions, they don't let you sleep peacefully in the bush," another boy continued.

"And the soldiers. We didn't know when they would come again."

"This place is safe," an older boy told the young ones. "And there is food here."

The youngest boy, about eleven, stretched himself, full length on his back under our tree, and put his hands behind his head like a pillow. "I wish my brother could see me now." He closed his eyes.

Habsa and I gossiped a bit with the women, as much as their strength would allow. We gave them and the boys a little cornmeal porridge from our own stores.

"Take this now, just this much," we told them. "It will keep you for the night. Tomorrow your belly will be able to take more."

Though it was early still, and the sun was not yet close to the horizon, the boys were ready to bed down. Their happiness gave way to sleep.

Suddenly the murmur of tired voices throughout the camp that late afternoon was broken by a shouting match.

"Wait, just wait!" a camp woman shouted in warning.

"The corn's still too hard!" another woman cried.

A group of starving men were closing in near the boiling pots, crowding and jostling the women tending the fire. "Let us through. We are hungry!" But the women locked arms and held their ground. The men were too weak to break through.

"The corn's raw still. It will be ready tomorrow. Stand back. It will make you sick."

"What do you mean—tomorrow?"

But now the group of new arrivals pressing in around the pots was growing, with women now and children, too, straining to look in, pushing. Seeing this, the cooking women tightened their own circle, putting their own flesh between the hungry and the fire.

"Do not try to eat it like this. Give us time to cook it through."

Then one boy slipped between their legs and lunged toward the pot.

Nyjang yelled at him, "Get back from there! That water's boiling!"

Another cooking woman grabbed him, "You wait!"

But the boy struggled. "If I wait, someone will take it before me!" he pulled against the woman's grip.

Then a very thin girl, who had been watching from behind the men, shot through like a snake, put her hand in the boiling water, took a handful of hot corn and put it in her mouth.

Then the boy broke free. "You can't stop me!" and he reached in and grabbed some hot corn too.

"You can't stop any of us!" said a man and broke through the weakened line.

Now it was too late, there was no more holding them back.

"Give me some!"

"Let me through!"

Then there were bodies wedging in from every side and hands fighting like piranhas in the boiling pots.

"Aaauuuhhh! My hand!"

"Get back!"

"There's nothing left for me!"

"Aayyyy! My mouth!"

Habsa grabbed a woman to stop her, "Your skin! It's going to burn!"

"What's my skin when my belly's empty?" the woman said, pushing Habsa aside.

And the people kept pushing through and filling their hands and their mouths with the steaming grains of dried corn. Even the cooking women were getting burned now too, as the pots tipped and the boiling water splashed.

Though no one could stop them, it didn't take long before one by one, these poor people dropped to their knees, vomiting. Vomiting until all the corn they'd forced down their throats came out. Vomiting until they could no longer stay upright on their knees. Vomiting until, as they lay there, the pain of the burns started to reach their minds, and they begged us for water to cool their hands, their arms and their tongues.

We stayed with them, then, into the evening, telling them again and again that they were safe now and that they should sleep and that it would be better for them in the morning.

8

BOYS TO MEN

If you shoot a zebra in the black stripe, the white goes, too.

ALL IN ALL, ABOUT TWO HUNDRED PEOPLE ARRIVED THAT DAY. OF those, only these lost control. The rest accepted a little water and laid down to sleep. We did not sleep, though. We were keeping watch now over the boiling water and grinding more corn for tomorrow.

There was a large intake shelter in our part of the camp. It had a tented roof and a packed mud floor. Here, some refugees could put down temporarily. Whoever had strength would build straw huts for themselves and move out of the shelter. The weaker ones would continue there or with relatives they found. The seriously ill would be taken to the camp hospital, to recover or to die.

The day after their arrival dawned cloudy and hot. For weakness the new ones lay resting well into the morning. But the women of the camp and some of the men rose early and began the work of the day, especially the work of this day, which would bear the weight of two hundred new refugees.

We gathered wood early. Nyjang found tea and boiled enough for many. Habsa and I boiled maize with clean water mixed with a little of the camp's milk powder. We looked for cups and tins to offer to our guests.

The happiness of the day before returned with the sun. The new arrivals were waking to find it was true that they were safe and among friendly Sudanese. By midmorning, the chatter of women and men and the light voices of children were filling up the air. There were very few cries of pain today. Voices of weeping flowed, instead, from tears of reunion.

The boys on the ground around my hut woke up smiling.

"Deng, get up, man, how are you?'

"Anwan, hey, how are you?" They woke each other with excitement.

I called them to join us and take some food. They scrambled to get up but I saw pain inside their bodies slowing down their movements. I guessed their full height was more than it seemed to be now as they walked bent over, careful, weak. But their voices were still strong.

"Hey, we made it, brother!" one slapped the other on the shoulder.

They sat down then, quite seriously, to eat. For a while there was no talking. They carefully took the tins from our hands and tasted the maize-water, holding their bodies still, giving time to their stomachs to accept the light food.

After a while, I asked them, "Where are you from?"

"A village in Bahr el Ghazal."

"Two of us. But Deng, he came later, on the way."

"Your village was attacked?" I asked.

"They came with horses. I am a young boy, but I see things and I understand."

"What did you see?"

"One week before, I was tending my father's cattle. I saw the soldiers come. They asked for the elders of the village."

"Take a little tea, also," Nyjang offered. The boy paused to consider if he could take it. He looked around at the others. One by one, they had all carefully accepted.

"They came to the elders in the afternoon. The next day everybody in the village was talking. The elders were mad."

"My father and my uncles were saying, 'We are Christians. We will stay Christians.' Then one night, in the early, early hours before sunlight, they came with horses."

"There was no time." He took a sip of tea water and waited. "My mother, my father, my sisters…there was no time. You hear gunshots. Someone is banging on the hut door with a rifle. You jump out of your window."

He put his cup down and started waving his arms. "Everyone, we just run in our own direction. If you look back for one second to find someone, you are dead. The next day we counted to see who is alive and who is killed. I could not find my little brother."

Other new arrivals were pulling themselves up around the camp. They were moving slowly but more easily, taking water from the hands of their hosts. All around there were new faces, new voices, and feelings of relief mixed with grief and sickness.

Dut sat with the girl child. He could not get her to play with him, so he just sat a while next to her, calling her attention and trying to make her smile.

"It was difficult for you," Habsa spoke while the boys were sipping their tea water and waiting for their strength to come again for more talking.

They were happy, but so weak and so young, no more than eleven, thirteen. Only the tallest one seemed older. I was twenty-one. But I felt a mother to them.

Out of the corner of my eye, I saw Monydit step out of the hut into the sun. The voices of the boys had drawn him out. But the shock of the bright light got him. He coughed and swore. That caught the boys' attention, and then their eyes would not move from him. His army pants, the only piece of clothing he had to wear since he arrived, raised him to hero status in their eyes. Their feeling was reflected in their silence. When their conversation started up again, it had a new theme.

"Just let me get a rifle. I'm gonna join the SPLA. Then I will fight those…." The boy made his voice louder, so that Monydit could hear.

"Me, too. When I'm in the SPLA, I'll have my rifle and I'll go back to my village. I will defend my mother and my sisters. I will kill anyone who comes close to them."

"I heard the SPLA will take you. Even if you are twelve...."

"I heard eleven. They come to the camps and they look for boys who can fight. If they come here, I'm going with them!" All the boys agreed.

Monydit stayed back from them, listening, silent. He washed his face and hands, then face again. He caught my eye and shook his head.

HABSA SURPRISED ME WHEN SHE WHISPERED IN MY EAR FROM BEHIND.

"Abuk, Ayen is in labor and she's having a hard time." Ayen was fifteen. She had lost her first child months before it could be born. The doctor had told her not to get pregnant again.

"Where is she?"

"She's in her hut right now. I'm going to be with her. Can you stay with the boys?"

"Yes, go on to Ayen. Just come back as soon as you can get away and tell me how she is doing."

"I will." She turned to go.

By now Monydit had reached where we were. These days he was getting stronger. And with the strength of his voice and body coming back, the goodness of his heart was finding ways to come out.

He settled down among the boys as I was finishing up.

"Was it hard for you coming here?" he asked the boys.

The presence of an SPLA soldier made the boys sit up and pull closer together.

He repeated his question, "I am Monydit. I stay over there." Their eyes followed the direction of his extended arm. "Was it a long trip? Did you have a hard time?"

"We walked three months."

"On the way, sometimes we just ate leaves, if we could find them."

"Was there water?"

"No. No water for a long time."

I offered Monydit some maize and some tea. He accepted it with thanks. The boys continued, "But one day on the road we saw a cow dead, for how long we didn't know."

The shorter boy spread out his hands to show the size of it. "It was big, but it was just bones and hide." They were only talking to Monydit now, expecting a better response from him than from the women.

"Oh, everybody jumped on that dead cow and cut the skin off its bones."

"And that cowskin was tough as this!" The short boy leaned back and pointed to the bottom of his foot. "Any other day we would have made it into shoes."

The taller boy continued, "But that day, we spent the whole afternoon chewing."

He demonstrated this for Monydit until they were all laughing.

"That was hunger," the tall boy concluded, pointing to his jaw. "But that," he pointed to his foot, "was not food."

"Some people died."

They got quiet for a moment, thinking, but still keeping Monydit as their center of thought.

"If the SPLA asks us, we will go and fight with them." The tall one spoke directly to Monydit, expecting approval, waiting for support.

Monydit dodged his words. "How many people escaped with you?"

The short boy answered, "Maybe a hundred, maybe three hundred. I don't know. Other people from other villages were joining us on the way when their villages were attacked, too."

Monydit was beginning to look like the first day I met him, keeping his breathing under control, holding himself in. I interrupted.

"Monydit, could you help me with Dut? I need to tend the fire here. He is in the hut."

Monydit rose slowly, "Yes, of course. Maybe I will stay with him a while."

He excused himself. As he neared the hut, I expected to hear him let out more coughing. He only leaned against the door and let out a long sigh.

The newly arrived woman and her child were sitting with us, listening too; they both had been quiet, the girl half closing her eyes. They did not seem unhappy, only silent. I filled a jar with tea and offered it to the woman.

"Have more tea. It is not hot. I've let it cool down. Please take some."

She received the clay jar I handed her with both hands and held it there.

"You are not thirsty?" I asked.

"I am remembering," she said.

In the distance, close to the big tent shelter, I saw some UN workers and camp volunteers setting up tables to register the rest of the arrivals. They would be asking their names, their hometowns, their ages. They would ask about their health. They would give them basic clothes.

"Are you from the boys' region?" I asked her.

"No, we joined the group later, one month before they crossed the river."

"Why do you hold the cup like that? Please drink something."

"To hold a cup, it is a great thing."

The short boy sighed deeply as he stretched his thin body on the warm, caked mud. The UN would give him pants later.

"May I hold your daughter?" I asked. She surrendered her child to my arms and sat back.

"I knew a woman on the way," she said. "She was carrying a baby. Her firstborn."

"Was she from your town?"

"Yes, she was. And she had a clay jar to hold milk."

"She brought it with her?"

"Yes, in the night when they attacked she escaped with her own life, her baby and a clay jar."

"She was lucky."

"Yes. Then in the days that followed, as we moved on, she would take that jar into the villages we passed. And whenever there was a family with a cow she would ask them to just put a little milk in the jar for her child. When there was no cow, she would ask in the same way for water, because the town people could never give to you unless you had a jar. So that clay jar became the secret of life for her and for her child along the way."

"This woman was smart."

"Yes. But one day the clay jar dropped from her hand onto the road. And a man, oh, the poor man, he didn't see it and he stepped on it."

"Oh, God."

"And broke it."

I saw Habsa come quickly out of Ayen's hut toward us.

"From that day on she had no way to get milk or water for her child."

The little girl now stirred in my arms. With my eyes I asked the woman if she could take the child back. She put the jar to one side, still looking after it. She told me, "If you want help you need to keep your own jar, even if it's empty for a long time."

The woman was used to a different flow of time, where a day's length is the same as a month's, where nothing starts and nothing ends. But for me a day had dimensions, a kind of rise and fall with turns and better paths and worse paths.

It was now the time of day for me to boil water and grind corn and gather more wood for fire. And Habsa was heading this way and waving with her hand that I should come.

"Please forgive me. There is work I must do."

"Let me help you. I have to learn the way you do things here."

"No, not now. Later, when you have more strength."

As if my chores would wait for strength!

I left the woman and her child to rest. The childbirth of my friend Ayen was filling my worries now. When Habsa saw me stand, she turned and hurried back to Ayen's hut. I followed. The day's regular work would have to wait.

Inside the walls of her own mud hut, Ayen was struggling to deliver the life of her child. I stooped to come in.

"Habsa, how is she doing?"

"She becomes hot and then cold."

The swelling in Ayen's feet and legs and hands was now extreme. Her face, known for its sweet and pleasant features, was blurred too by the awful swelling.

Habsa spoke up. "Ayen, Abuk is here." She gave no response, but pulled her knees up in the bed.

"Ayen," I took her hand, "How are you doing?" She did not answer, but her breathing steadied. Yom was also here with us.

"Habsa, what happened to her?"

"She was having pains and pushing hard, and everything was going ok. Then on the last push she got one terrible pain high up in her belly. She screamed and started bleeding rivers. The child has pulled back up into her. Here you can feel him."

It was true. I could feel his backbone high up under her skin, below her ribcage, where her stomach should be.

Then another contraction came, and Ayen cried out and shook. More blood came. I held her hand tighter now, for the pain to drain off into me.

"We have to get her to the hospital, Abuk."

"But who will help carry her? Her husband has gone with the SPLA. The new refugee boys are still too weak."

Yom said, "We'll get a sheet, and Habsa and I will carry her."

"It's too long a walk. We will not make it."

"Then someone will help us on the way. We have to go." Yom found a tarp to put her friend on.

"Abuk, my young cousin Deng will help us. He is coming now. Here, help me with this."

We spread the tarp out long ways next to Ayen. We braced ourselves and rolled her slowly to one side pushing the tarp little by little under her. Her teeth were chattering. Deng burst in. "What can I do, auntie?" He was a boy of about twelve. He had been too sick to join SPLA that spring, but he was better now and willing to help in everything.

"Deng, take this end," Yom told him. He took the end of the tarp where Ayen's head was cradled and bundled it to make a handhold.

Yom and Habsa took hold of the ends by her feet. Ayen's body was convulsing now and pulling against them.

"Ayen, be still now. We are taking you. Abuk, you go back and care for the new people. We are going." Habsa motioned with her free hand. Deng backed out the door, gripping his end. Habsa and Yom followed, with Ayen's blood filling the tarp and dripping onto the earth between their feet.

"Come soon and tell me how she does," I said. Habsa nodded as she kept pace with the others, her hands gripping the tarp, her eyes set on Ayen. "Ayen, we have you," She said. "We have you." They cleared the huts quickly and turned onto the road.

LATER IN THE DAY, SOME OLDER SUDANESE MEN FROM THE CAMP came to talk with the newly arrived boys.

"Do you see the clouds?" they told the boys. "The rains are coming. You must prepare."

It was true. The sky had been darkening and the temperature of the camp had dropped. Everyone knew that when you felt the cold wind, the rains would surely follow. That was the certainty of things.

Out of the corner of my eye I saw Habsa and Yom, returning from hospital, entering the hut of my friend Ayen.

The men continued, "We will bring you with us and show you where to get wood and grass and how to build huts for yourselves."

The boys had been on the road two or three months without food and had taken their first taste of clean water yesterday and of maize only today. The tallest boy raised his chin and answered, "Thank you, we will come with you."

But I told the men, "If it rains tonight, we will take the boys into our own huts. Last night they slept all around us on the open ground. Tonight we will take them in."

The men looked to the oldest man among them to respond. He was a friend of Nyjang and her husband. "Abuk, you already have the woman and her child with you, and your husband's cousin and your own boy. Your hut is small. And the other huts, they are small, too."

"There is always room, uncle. We will make room."

The lead man got up to leave. "That is good for now," he said. The others rose, too. "But remember, the boys must build their own hut, and they must do it soon, before the floods."

After the men went on their way, I washed my hands with the last of the clean water and shared it with the boys so they could wash, too. I cleared away the uneaten maize to give the boys space to rest. I refreshed the fire and placed more water on it to boil. It was too late to wash clothes now, but I could grind some corn before night fell. But in the back of my mind was the question, *Why hasn't Habsa come to bring me news?*

9

THE WISDOM OF CHILDREN

Even the tallest mountain begins in the ground.

A TURN OF THE WIND BROUGHT THE ANSWER TO MY EARS. IT WAS THE voice of weeping, coming from the hut of Ayen. On its heels the voice of thunder also spoke. The storm was close. As the wind picked up, I stirred the boys and called to the woman, who was already gathering up her child. Big drops of rain began to fall.

"You," I called to the short boy, "Go into my hut. Follow the woman and her child."

"You," I called to the tallest boy, "Take the others with you and look for people who can take you in."

More and more rain was falling. The new arrivals all over the camp were rising to their feet, and the kinder people of the camp were calling them to come into their huts or were taking them to people who they thought might take them in. The rain was hitting hard. Between the claps of thunder came the drumming of the spring rain striking the tin tubs, pelting the tin roofs of the latrines, carpeting the camp with rippling, deepening mirrors of pooled water. It doused my open fire.

But underneath it all I heard the swelling voice of weeping. Habsa and Yom, urged on by the storm, were crying out louder and louder now. As soon as I saw my guests were settled, I ran through the rain to Ayen's hut.

Ayen had died quickly in the UN hospital. The doctor said only surgery could save her. They were not equipped. She was too young. Her second pregnancy had come too soon. Her young womb had torn. Too much blood was lost. Where was her husband? Fighting. In what place? There's been no news of him for months. Was he still alive? No one knew. Her body they'd bring back tomorrow for burial.

All night we women wept and sang for her with the storm, the sky's tears bigger than ours. For her child I could not weep much. It now slept in the loving grave of Ayen's womb. Ayen and her child had left the camp together, joined forever, and would be okay now. Tradition urged me to weep, but my heart whispered between the thunderclaps that for them all would be well.

These days of reunion at the arrival of the of travelers had been happy ones. We did not want our sadness for our friend to spread, so we shared it just among ourselves.

We healed through the night and greeted the next day well. The sky had also healed up and was now bright and clear.

THE ORPHANED BOYS STIRRED AT SUNRISE.

"Angok, get up, man!"

"I'm up! You get Achol!"

"We have to find the men who came by yesterday."

"It's a good day to build a hut."

The boys were ready to begin their work. They would need to eat and drink. But after the long night, my strength was drained away.

"Koich, can you help me?" I had learned the name of the tallest boy.

"Yes, auntie, tell me what to do." So this morning, with his help, the fire was built, the maize and water gruel was boiled, the tea was set. He showed no shame in helping me.

"Koich, last night there was too much rain. We did not have a good place for you."

"Auntie, don't worry about it. We are just glad we are in a safe place."

More than the usual number of boys was gathering for breakfast. Maybe the sight of their friend cooking had drawn them. He was breaking tradition.

"Koich, I know the rain was cold."

"Believe me, auntie, we are happy here."

The shorter boy stepped closer to join in.

"And the rain, auntie, it is a good sign. Rain is love from God."

I saw men beginning to gather outside of Ajwong's hut as they always did about this time of day. I could hear the hissing of the voices on his transistor radio mixed with the angry voices of the listening men. Many of those men had been chased here by the northern army. They lived with fear that government soldiers would cross the border and come here to find them and kill them.

These men were never at ease. They would sit on the heels of their feet, ready to jump at any time. When they talked to you, they were looking behind you; when you talked to them, they were listening not to you but to other sounds, sounds in the bush, sounds in the camp, and sometimes the footsteps of people no one could see.

"Auntie, may we start to eat now?"

The boys were all looking at me, waiting. I quickly passed bowls to them. "Please, take some maize and tea. Today you have to eat more. Please."

The woman who had carried the child into camp joined us. The girl child was now walking a little, and the woman had more life in her. She would take some food, too. She sat down next to me.

"How was your night?" I asked her.

"Good, thank you."

Koich was already in front of her with a bowl full of the watery breakfast and in his other hand a metal tin with tea. He held out both to her. "Would you like some maize? I helped to make it this morning!" She accepted them carefully, keeping the hard tin far from the girl's forehead.

He asked her, "Do you remember that praying man on the road?" Now I was learning about Koich. When he was happy, oh, how he would talk.

"Yes, I do. That man he prayed for everything!" Now this was the first smile I saw on the face of that woman.

"I learned to pray too, from watching him." Koich was already a wise man, though still mostly a boy. "Whenever he needed something, he would ask God."

The woman added what she knew, "He told me he was in England for a while. He went to school there. And then he came back to Sudan and got married and had a child. And then the war caught him."

Koich continued, "I met him one day when we were passing him and his neighbors on the narrow road. He had already been walking a long time with his wife and child. That's when I spent time with him —before we passed on and left them back.

"He told us how there was no food or water for a long time on the road. So he just kept walking and praying because he was too tired to worry. He told his wife, 'We're too weak. God must help us now.'"

The woman added, "He told us that just then a man came out of a village and invited them in and let them eat."

Koich continued, "This man told me to just be quiet and walk and pray and then say thank you when help comes.'"

The shorter boy argued, "But you don't just fall in the river and say 'God will help me!' You've got to swim. Because it's easier for God if you are a good swimmer." Koich laughed and pushed the boy over.

From the corner of my eye I saw women gathering with the men around the radio outside Ajwong's hut. Every day about this time, whoever had a chance went there to hear what was happening in the war. But Koich still wanted to talk.

"Auntie, I was not used to walking like that. My feet swelled up and hurt and I was so tired. Back home I used to stay with the cattle and watch them and keep the lion away. That was my job in the village. But to walk all night and never stop walking...days and days and days and with no food. I was so tired."

"Koich, I am sorry to hear it."

"But all the people were encouraging me. 'Be strong. Be brave. We will make it.' It is the courage of the people walking with me that made me reach this place."

"I think you are brave too."

"No, that's not it. The older ones kept telling me, 'We are almost there, Koich, one more day.' I believed them, even though they said that every day for two months until we got here."

One by one the boys finished breakfast and lay back down close to the cooking pot, with their bowls gripped in their hands. I didn't know how they would build huts today. Their bodies needed more time than their minds to recover.

I motioned to invite the new woman to come with me to hear the radio at Ajwong's hut. But she leaned back against the tree and closed her eyes, cradling the girl child in her arms.

Habsa caught my eye from across the circle. She put down her things. "Abuk, come with me. We have a few minutes. Let's hear the news."

Everyone was pressing in to hear the radio, like wild dogs jostling for a scrap of meat. One man looked up when we approached. "Abuk, he's about to start. Sit here."

"No, thank you, uncle. I will stand." This man was nearing fifty. That was old age in the camp. He had fought in both wars and was scarred on his face and arms. In the camp he walked limping, a bullet still lodged in his thigh, living his defeat every day—except when he sat with the men by the radio.

It was this way for a lot of the men. When they heard the voice of the SPLA, defeat stopped for them, because on the radio the war was different. On the radio it was under control. On the radio it was a game of strategy and chance, to be won by the clever and agile. On the radio war was a man's sport with winners, not a death march with losers on all sides.

I stood there watching the men's excitement as they listened to my husband's heartening stories over the wire. His voice today, as always, was fine and clear.

Like every day, the war I fought was against my own heart. He sounded well-fed, self-satisfied, and strong. As always, his tone told

me that in Addis Ababa he did not feel defeat and in Addis Ababa he
was lacking nothing. Habsa stood close by me today, "Your husband
is doing well," she said in a low voice.

But there was a battle of questions in me. *He's brought us to this
place. And now he's fine and we are not. Why is this? Why?*

Standing by the radio with everyone, the anger I felt was too
much to let me stay. I walked back to my hut remembering to be
loyal. *It is wrong to think this way. It helps no one.* And now the boys
were stirring again. I needed to teach them to get water to wash
themselves.

"Auntie Abuk, tomorrow we will go with the men to build huts."

"That's good, Koich." *You have a good heart. I do not have such
a good heart today.*

"Tell me how you built your hut, auntie. It is a beautiful one."

"It's too much to tell." *How far is it to Addis? I could go by car.*

"Auntie...."

"The men will show you how to build much simpler ones."
Everyone loves my husband's voice but me.

"Then we will be done in one day!"

"It takes more than a day." *I have to talk to him.*

"Why, auntie?"

I wanted to stop his questions and to stop my thoughts. But both
kept coming.

"Because you must get water jugs and cooking pots, too, from the
UN Center if you can. And corn and oil. You will be cooking for
yourselves while you are building, and getting your own water."

"I remember a time, a long time on the road, when we had no
water," Koich continued. "No rain, no river, no water near the places
where we hid."

"I heard that people died along the way."

"There were two kinds of people walking with us on that road.
The way I see it, one kind died. One kind lived."

"How so?" *I want to be the kind who lives. I will teach it to
my boy.*

"There were people, when they got thirsty, they said to each other,
'Oh, I remember my water back home. It was sweet, and the well was

deep.' Those people said, 'We are here but water is back there.' When they fell down thirsty, they said, 'Oh, if I just could have one drop of the water from that well.' And they died like that."

"And you did not say things like that?"

"I learned from the other kind of people who said, 'Maybe we'll get water in the next village,' or 'I think there's a river up ahead.' When I was with them they put a picture in my mind of the next place with water."

"But you are also young. That helped. You had the strength to walk."

"Some other boys who started out as strong as me, they died on the way."

"You were very lucky."

"It was not luck that made me strong. It was the pictures in my mind."

When he said that, I felt ashamed.

"Then, Koich, you have to pray for me, because the pictures in my mind are not good ones."

"Auntie Abuk, whatever you need, ask God for it. And if it's something you really need, say 'I will get it, I will get it.' And, definitely, you will!" Koich was certain he had been brought to the gates of heaven when he landed here with us.

So in those days I began to pray more, day and night. When I stepped out of my bed, I asked that there would be no snake; when I went to the latrine I asked God that it not fall in; when I cooked our food I asked for food tomorrow, and when I looked at my son I said my biggest prayer, "Oh God, please let him live...." I prayed every time of every day for everything. And always, in everything, I asked, "Please, don't let me lose hope." Because a person without hope is a rusted lamp without oil.

And when I prayed like this, it seemed that things were changing. If we needed something, someone would come by with it. If I had a question in my heart, someone or something would answer it.

But the answer to my biggest prayer would not come. Monydit was getting stronger, but Dut kept getting weaker.

One morning, while I was putting cracked wood on the morning fire, setting the water to boil, counting the grains of corn and thinking how I would stretch them, Monydit called out.

"Abuk! Abuk! Come!"

When I turned, I saw just the heel of his foot as he disappeared into our hut. I followed and saw him bent over Dut's mat. Dut's back was arched like the back of a starving dog, tight, ribs raised.

"Abuk, he won't breathe!"

"Monydit, turn him, roll him over. Hit his back!"

We rubbed his back and slapped it with our open palms and called his name and squeezed his chest. Little by little Dut came back to us.

"Monydit, I'm taking him to the hospital!"

"I will watch the water then. Don't think behind you. Just go."

In a few seconds I was passing through the huts and toward the road. I ran by Habsa's hut and told her I would not be in the circle today. When I got to the high road, I heard her footsteps behind me.

This road was the only way when the camp was flooded. It was narrow but higher than the land around. As we hurried, the sounds of camp life became less behind us, but ahead we heard a sound of weeping. I recognized a juncture coming up that was near the hospital. There we would turn onto the main road.

As we approached the crossing, I saw a woman standing there, carrying a child too. She had wrapped him like I'd wrapped Dut. It was her voice that we had heard a long way off. She was headed toward the camp.

Once we were face to face. I asked her,

"Have you been to hospital?"

"Yes," she replied.

"Why are you crying?"

"My son is dead!"

Habsa stepped forward, to come between me and the woman.

"And I have no one to bury him. I don't know what to do!"

The woman turned to show me her dead baby.

"No!" When I cried out, I felt my son lift his head to see. I had covered him, but now he was looking at that lady and at the dead child in her arms. He would not put his head back down. The woman rocked the dead child and held him close.

Habsa stayed between me and the woman and spoke to her, "Woman, go on back to camp. The men there will help you. You will be all right." After more words from Habsa, she got quiet and turned and continued down the road.

Maybe I will go to the hospital, and my son will die too. And what then? Will I look like her?

As we walked on, Habsa talked to God, "Lord, help that woman, let her be strong." She talked to me too. "Abuk, put peace in your heart. Nothing will happen to Dut."

I could feel Dut straining to see over my shoulder back down the road after the child. I thanked God for the life I could feel in him. Whether I believed my friend's promise or not, I kept walking.

Itang is a place where there's no happiness at all. Every morning you get up and you don't do anything benefiting your future. You just get up and look for food and you eat. And you wash your hands with soap and go to sleep. Everything costs your energy. You have to think, "If I do this, energy goes, but if I don't do this, nothing comes."

Many times the doctors had saved my son's life. We believed they would do that today.

The camp hospital was a low building with a few open rooms. It was crowded inside and out today. People lay on every side, inside and outside on the higher ground under a walkway roof, up against the walls, under the trees. A few people stood. I crossed the yard, passing ahead of several sick and dying, stepping around some, over some. I rushed inside the hospital and found an attendant.

"Please, sir, take us to see Dr. Steven! Please, sir! Dr. Steven!"

It was midday. The attendant showed me three different lines, one for this doctor and one for the other doctor and one for Dr. Steven.

"There are two hundred people waiting here, ma'am. The hospital has twenty beds, and they are full. No one is well. Take your son to the end of that line."

The line followed the wall, down the long hallway, and trailed out through the door far out into the courtyard.

"Dr. Steven is on duty and he will see you when it's your turn."

"No!" I cried out loud, "I must see him right away!"

"I'm sorry."

The attendant turned away. Habsa pulled me back, through the door, out into the courtyard. By now I was crying.

From the beginning of the lines to the end, the sick were collapsed against this wall or lying in the dirt, covered with flies, coughing, vomiting, doubled over. We took our place outside at the end of Dr. Steven's line.

Two hours passed, and we were still in the same spot. In the third hour the line moved up because someone ahead had died and his family removed him.

I held Dut and talked to him, suddenly his back and arms went loose. I held him tighter to see if I could feel him breathe. I called him, I shook him, "Dut, don't leave me. Dut! Breathe!" I called him until he opened his eyes. But the line did not move.

The UN hospital had always been a place of hope for me. Every doctor there was good and kind. They had given me back my son alive so many times. It had never been a place of death for me. It had never been a place of fear for me until today.

A refugee camp is not like any other place on earth. It is like a Halloween place, because you see things that are not normal at all. It's nothing like the life that you knew. The things you see here in one day would be enough. Even if you don't see those things, you hear a story. Whether you see the bad things with your eyes or see someone else's bad life in your mind, it is the same – today and then tomorrow and the next day, with not one good day in between. That is why the people get crazy here. You feel like someone who got condemned to punishment. How can a condemned person hope for something good?

When the sun was gone from the sky, Dr. Steven called to us and took us in.

He took one look at Dut. "The infection has gone too far. Dut must be injected now and again every four hours for the next two days or he will die. He must be hospitalized for this." *This is Dr. Steven. He knows what to do.*

"But, Abuk, the hospital is completely full. There is no room."

"We don't need a bed. We will lie on the floor here in the hall. Don't turn us away now, I'm not asking much...."

"I will send an attendant back to camp with you. He will give the injections and stay with you until Dut is better."

Dr. Steven gave the first injection to my son right there, before he was called to the emergency room. But, as promised, he sent a technician home after us to watch over Dut.

On the way home, I was too tired. My thinking was still not good. "Itang is like a burial place. It is not a living place. It is just a place where you take a person and leave him to die!" Habsa was tired too. Too tired to say it was not so.

Every four hours the hospital attendant came and injected antibiotics into Dut. After two days, the sickness stopped and Dut could breathe again like a normal child.

As soon as Dut was able to talk, his question was, "Mama, did that little child we saw on the road die?"

"Yes."

"What is the difference between him and me?"

"I don't know."

"Mama, I think God helped me."

I remember his words now, but at the time when he said them I was tired and the corn was not ground and the water was not boiled and the pots were not washed. Clouds were gathering for another rain, and in my mind the day ahead was going to be bad like all the days before.

As I had told Koich, the pictures in my mind were not good.

10

GHOST IN A SILK DRESS

Friendship doubles joy and halves grief.

"ABUK MAKUAC?"

By this time, I had become settled and even grateful for our circle of five cooking fires. In a hellish place one can still love and be loved. We had built up a rhythm of business, scraping together our UN corn and oil, trading what we had with outlying villagers for better food, saving together, planning together, crying and singing our songs together. When food was scarce, gratitude for this kept me feeling safe enough to want to live another day.

"Abuk Makuac? They told me this is the hut of Abuk Makuac."

A man dressed in the dark green of SPLA stood over me at the cooking fire where I was boiling the water I'd brought back last night from the river.

"Yes, it is."

His body blocked the barely risen sun. I could not see his face at first, just the outline of a broad-brimmed hat.

"Are you Maker Benjamin's wife?"

The milk I'd bought with profits from oil and corn stood waiting, and a tiny piece of meat I'd also bought for Dut would not last long in the heat uncooked. Our stomachs were empty.

"Yes."

"Your husband calls for you. Get your things ready." He squatted down to talk to me eye to eye. "It's me." There was a smile in his voice. "Did you forget me?" As he turned the sun shone on his face.

"Selva? Selva Kiir? You are here! How are you?" I straightened my dress and reached up to pull back my hair. The last time he'd seen me up close was at the great Hotel D'Afrique. Now he had to ask if it was me.

"I am fine, Abuk. How are you?" He surveyed my rough hands and the rough ground around me and with his eye measured out the hut behind me. "Maker is calling for you. He wants to see you and his son."

"Where?"

"In Addis Ababa."

My friends needed me to cook what we'd gathered before the sun rose too high. Then Dut and I would eat and share with them. Then I would grind tomorrow's corn against the stone. Then we would find shade and rest a bit. This rhythm was as much a part of me as breathing. One does not stop breathing.

"The top commander gave orders to find you. I've come to bring men back with me for training. You will come with us."

The smell of warming tea was in the air, already lifting my heart for our morning greetings and bracing my heart for the day's heat and labor.

"Get ready, Abuk," he called over his shoulder. "By tomorrow night you will be with your husband in the best hotel in Addis!" He walked back into the dusty morning light but his shadow was long and the tip of it did not depart for a while.

Is my mind playing tricks on me?

But by late morning word had spread. Soon everyone was saying that another truck of men was leaving and that this time Dut and I would be on it.

I worked differently that day, gathering up my things. My thoughts turned slowly in this new direction. *How long will we be gone? I have to bathe myself and Dut and polish the inside of my hut one more time before we go. I have to ask someone to keep the hut as*

long as we are gone. What if we never come back? My heart skipped.
*I must give the few dresses relatives have sent me and my other things
to friends. I have to hurry.*

But now the belly pain that was always with me, a sign that something bad was growing, was begging me to stop. *I need help. Where is
my bag? What do I even have to put in it? Yom has taken Dut to play,
so my hands are free but my mind is bound.*

"Abuk?" Habsa, was at the door. "Do you need some help?"

She joined me in gathering my things to keep them safe from rats
and floods while away. *There are things I want to say to her but I
need help gathering my words too.*

*How can I leave my closest friend? Who will walk with her to the
river? Who will know her heart and speak hope back to her in the
morning? Who will wail with her for the dead? Oh God—and who
will die while I am not here?*

*Tomorrow Habsa will still be here and hungry. I will not.
Tomorrow I will be where Maker has been all along.*

Anxiety and guilt and anger boiled over into tears when at last my
back was on my bed for sleep that night. In the camp, it is always the
one who leaves who cries the most.

Morning came too fast. How many times in the last year I'd
woken up inside this hut, with the light filtering in through the door,
through the crude hole we called a window, and here and there at
times the sun would come in through weak spots in the thatched roof.
How many times before going to market had I taken out my dimin-
ishing cache of jewelry and my last few silken dresses and spread
them before me one by one, to enjoy memories of better days and
then to decide which I would sell. By now my jewelry was all but
gone and I had only two of the dresses left that I had brought here
from Sudan. One was rose colored, one blue. I folded the rose one
with my photographs and passport in my travel bag. I laid the blue
one out.

The blue dress. That's the one I've kept so carefully. British
made, of silk, patterned with swirling flowers. That was the dress I
brought back home from England in August 1982, three months after
my first baby died. My sister-in-law had bought it for me to cheer me

and to give me hope. This dress I could not sell. Today it waited for me while I did a few chores with my friends. Then Selva Kiir found me with them and told me it was time to go. The truck was leaving. *Oh God, so soon!* I hurried back to my hut.

Though I'd touched and gazed upon my better clothes so many times here, I had not put any on. This was the first day in over twelve months I was going to wear one. I drew the blue dress up above my head to slip it on. And when it fell and slid down along my arms and face, draped itself loose around my shoulders and flowed like water down my back, the coolness of it brought back the brightness of my former life. But when it passed my hip bones and belly and almost slid off, everything felt wrong. I had no mirror. My friends were not here. I smoothed the material flat across my chest and down. My belly was an empty hollow place. My hips stuck out like jawbones. My dry, cracked hands and fingers snagged the threads along the soft silk. *Oh God, who am I?*

Shouts of happiness outside, loud voices calling out my name to come out brought me back. Dut was calling with them too. Light-headed, I turned to check the things I would leave behind. *How long will we be gone? How will we live? I need more time.* That's when darkness started pooling in my eyes like the rain that fills deep holes in a road, that's when my belly remembered its pain, and my neighbors' voices poured like cold water over me. The ground hit hard like rock against my shoulder.

The first hand I felt on my face was Dut's, his fingers opening my eyes, "Mama, Mama...."

I felt my friends cradle me and help me up. I felt them weep.

"She'll be better there. She will."

"Abuk, it's okay. Don't be afraid."

"Just remember us."

My voice promised. My hands held theirs. But my life had been rooted in the earth of the camp too long now and would not come with me. The officer sent to pick me up straightened when he saw me and respectfully opened the door of his jeep to me, bowing slightly. He didn't know that the person who got in the car with him was only a ghost in a silk dress.

THAT WAS THE BEGINNING OF A NEW TIME IN MY LIFE. THINGS WERE changing. But I didn't know for better or for worse.

After hours on a bumpy road, our caravan stopped in Gambella. There, I began to feel the nature of the change. President John Garang himself ordered that my son and I fly in his own helicopter with him and his party to Addis. I was to be looked after, accompanied, and granted privilege and care.

It was a strange thing to be suddenly lifted up and separated from the earth and see the surrounding countryside from high above, like through the eyes of a bird. I wondered if, when our dead looked down, that this was what they saw. Green rolling hills, green spreading fields—tiny animals leaping and little men walking and small huts scattered out among the trees. That dangerous and rugged land from up here looked serene, luxurious.

Inside the cabin of the helicopter the knots of my stomach untied a little as I heard the voices of the other passengers talking above the din of the machine. Just hearing their words in my language and seeing them there, sitting so calm—it was a help to me.

Soon John Garang became concerned about my son. He decided he would make Dut laugh, and laugh he did, many times, even though his eyes were infected and crusty. He couldn't open the right one. John Garang teased him,

"Open your eyes, little boy, and see this pretty country!" And Dut rubbed his eyes and did it just for him.

The place we landed must have been a military base. It was rough and dusty and I saw only soldiers. I could not see a city anywhere near. As we deplaned, John Garang disappeared into the back of a black car. I did not see him again for many months.

Another driver appeared, put our things into his car, and invited me and my son to get in. He drove rough roads, then straight into Addis Ababa, then right and left through the city streets. Soon the driver left us with our bag in a large hotel lobby. I recognized the place. It was the great Hotel d'Afrique of our first time in Ethiopia.

But when did this hotel become so imposing, so loud? When did its lights become so blinding? I did not remember there being so many people last time, such shrill languages, so many feet.

There were a few guests whom I thought I recognized, as I waited for what might happen next.

Then I saw Maker. I spotted him first, in his ever-pressed dark pants and white shirt, waiting by the desk; his polished shoes and high forehead flashed in the crystal light. I watched him scan the crowd, his eyes skipping quickly over us again and again as he looked for me among the well-dressed women arriving. Then at last my long stare caught him.

When he finally recognized me, I saw in his sudden big smile and brightened eyes, that this day was as big for him as it was for me. By the time we reached each other, Dut was jumping and we were all three of us so happy, we couldn't let go of each other for the longest time. There was pain, but there was also joy. I let it come. Then he brought us up the broad stairs, me leaning on him, Dut in his arms, and let us into our room.

It had been a long time since my feet had touched a carpet. The rug was thick and welcoming; I left my old shoes at the door. On my right, the bed was broad and perfect, cloaked with tapestry. All around, the lamps, the picture frames, the chairs were exquisite—intelligently made. The open window looked out over city streets and farther down into a red horizon. I inhaled the sweetness of freshly starched air and glanced toward the full-length mirror on the closet door.

I saw our poor, hard-working maid reflected in it. Pity flashed from my heart to her. The woman's hair was dusty and small on her head and she had such a sad look. All this I caught in the first glance as my heart went out to her.

But on my second look, a shock went through me. The woman was my height, she wore my dress, and when I moved, she did the same. *Oh God, this is me! Look at me. Look at me. I am a ghost, an ugly ghost.*

"Abuk, you and Dut will stay here." Maker was with him at the sink, washing his eyes. Now he was holding Dut at the window, showing him the sights and teaching him names for things he'd never seen before.

I studied myself silently in the mirror. My eyes were big and dull like the eyes of an abandoned dog. There was no radiance left at all in my dark skin to call out the brightness of my dress or to glisten with even one ray of light from the crystal in this room. And my hair, where was my hair? Had I been so sick I'd lost my hair? How could anybody love me like this, with so little hair?

"Mommy?" Dut was trying on his daddy's shoes. "Look at me!" He rushed to shuffle forward toward me.

"Dut, honey." He tripped and tumbled toward me, laughing and laughing. While he lay at my feet carelessly pushing his fingers into the deep weave of the carpet, I saw something flash across his eyes, "Pepsi, Mommy. I want Pepsi!"

I told him that I would bring him water, but Maker said, "Abuk, the SPLA pays for our meals here. He can have anything he wants. How about some dinner?"

"No, Maker, please. Not yet." The only thing I wanted to do now was lie down, just lie down. "You go ahead."

"But you need to eat."

"I'll have water now. But you can bring something back for Dut later."

So my husband unpacked a few things for us, kissed us both, and left. I lay on the broad bed for a long time with Dut curled up beside me. The smell of new soap drifted in from the bathroom. There is clean water here and perfumed soap and soft cream for our skin. There are fresh towels. I want to bathe. I want to wash my face and my hair. I want to wash off all the dust from my son and from myself.

Thinking this, I fell asleep and dreamed of the rivers of southwest Sudan, sparkling as they moved under broad green trees, watering the land and bringing with them fish and great birds. I dreamed of the tree-lined streets in my hometown and of the spring rains. Of the tall stone wall protecting our house. The flower garden and the grounds within, filled with aunts and uncles, cousins, my grandparents, neighbors. Then I saw the rains fall harder, forming torrents churning through the streets. Suddenly the flood was a swirling river of

animals and men and children, houses and cattle and women struggling to pull free. It widened when it reached my father's house and
sucked everything in. I was being pulled in too, but I would not let
go. I would not let go. I woke up soaked in my own sweat.

The hotel room was dark now. A breeze was lifting up the curtains
from the open window glass. That felt good on my wet skin. I spoke
out loud, "Dut is with me. This bed is strong. These walls are thick.
We are safe, and Maker will come back." As I spoke, Dut opened his
eyes and pulled closer to me.

After this, for the next few days, though Maker was in another
place, he had room service bring meals to me and Dut. They brought
us juices and fresh water, rice, cooked eggs, and *injera*, my native
bread. The food was nothing like the hard corn of the camp. It was
soft and fresh and warm, and my stomach remembered how to accept
it. Then I asked Maker if he could bring me clothes and nice shoes so
we could go out. I wanted to see the city. The bad dreams came at
night, but the days were bright. My heart would have to find a way to
make peace between the two.

On the fourth day, Maker came early.

"Are you ready, Abuk? I want to show you the market. We'll get
clothes for you there."

He brought me down to the hotel lobby and walked me on his arm
across its palatial floor. Then with me on one side of him and Dut on
the other, he took us out onto the broad, smooth streets to show us the
bustling markets.

"Abuk, everything you could want, they are selling here."

There were people from every country around us. Well-dressed
men and pretty women passed us—Ethiopians, wealthy Somalis,
light-skinned Arabs, West Africans, and even Europeans, with their
pale skin and fine clothes, opening their wallets to the vendors. A
family from India passed near us, too, with little ones, a wife, and a
husband, accompanied by an aging, beautifully dressed woman, who
walked behind them. She was examining the goods in this shop and
that, speaking loudly to him in a strange tongue, gesturing and
complaining. The streets smelled of curry and goat cheese, sweet
incense and perfume.

Today in this place, I felt myself coming back to another part of me. I pulled my feelings and my thoughts together, "Someone cared for me and brought me here. I am with healthy and respected people. Some of them know me. Now I am sure that I have survived."

"Abuk, look over here." Maker was turning to look into one shop. I saw brightness in his eyes. "They sell pretty things here. Let's stop." Maker is a man who smiles like a boy when he's happy.

"Look at this, Abuk." His smile was as deep as the great carved bowl he was pointing to. It was the kind of bowl that a family would sit around and eat from all together. We turned it over and over, admiring the feel of it while Dut stood happily squeezed in between us. Maker and I stood close for a long time in that shop, admiring many things. That day, my tender feelings for my husband grew. That day, our marriage love was starting up again, and the anger I felt toward him in the camp was fading.

THERE WERE OTHER SPLA WIVES IN THE HOTEL, TOO. THE WIVES OF General Kerubino and their children. The wife of General Aronton. And there were others. From the first day on I met often with all of them. We would gather ourselves together every day and put our kids together in each other's rooms and just sit and talk and have tea. Life was almost perfect, and for those few days I stopped crying for myself and only cried for the people who were still in the war back home or in the camp. I remembered them in my heart and whenever we talked about them in the hotel.

On the fifth day of my first week, the women gathered in my hotel room. It was their time to braid hair and take care of each other's beauty. They brought bags of brushes and combs and bright beads, nail polish and pumice stone, creams and sweet-smelling lotions. The big bed, the chairs in my room and the chairs they brought in, were enough to give everyone a place. They sat here and there, facing this way and that, talking, talking. The senior wife of Kerubino was there and two of his other wives. Some women had been in the camp earlier; others had come straight from the capital of Sudan. I was still learning their names, but their faces and voices were already home to me.

"Abuk, how are you enjoying yourself?" asked a tall woman, with dark, reddish skin.

"She was in Itang," another added.

"I know it is tough there," said a third.

"All the time in the camp, I only thought about my son." This was my honest answer.

"You had to worry about feeding him every day with nothing. I understand. That is very hard. I know it is very hard." The tall woman again.

Shiloh, a slight girl of twelve years, was weaving in and out among us, gathering up the younger children who were hitting each other with brushes and pocketing the beads like candy. "Shiloh, take the children to my room next door," the tall woman said.

"Yes, ma'am."

"And watch them carefully."

"Yes, ma'am." Dut's head was turning from her to me and back.

"Dut," I told him. "Go on with the other children." He did, and the door closed behind them.

The women turned back to me to continue their welcome and gentle questioning. This was their way.

I gladly answered them. "Really I was also worrying about what I would do when he was old enough for school."

"It is enough that a mother kills herself to feed her child, much less find him a school!" The senior wife of Kerubino spoke with authority.

"And you did a good job!" Encouraging voices were coming from everywhere.

"Look at him, Abuk. He is fat!"

"And look at you, you are just bones!"

"I am okay. But what if there is no school for him?" I still had this question, even in Addis.

"Anyway he will grow up strong." Kerubino's senior wife spoke the most when the women gathered. "And stay next to you and take care of the mother who fed him!"

"But what about school? When there is peace again in Sudan, if our children haven't gone to school, who will be the new leaders?"

"The men who have always been leaders." Another wife of Kerubino spoke.

"There is no lack of them," a young woman sitting by the window answered, but with some irony in her voice.

"They fight the wars. Then they become leaders," the wife continued with confidence. "And then they start up wars again."

"That is the problem," the tall woman interrupted.

"So, you are talking bad about our husbands."

"I am talking about all Sudan. We have a bad habit in Sudan. Somebody says, 'Oh, I don't like this situation.' And right away someone gets a gun and starts shooting."

"So?"

"Nobody says, 'Let's sit down and talk together.' Nobody says, 'What is the solution?'"

"We do! We women sit down; we talk together. We are their wives."

"But who listens to you?"

"They should listen."

"This is what I want my boy to learn," I spoke again. "To listen and to talk through things."

"Then he can learn from us!"

"But I want him to go to school."

"Where can he go to school? We are not welcome in Sudan or here or anywhere. The day may come when we are even chased away from here."

"Then he has to go to a school far away from here."

"Where?"

"I don't know. In a place where the leaders talk to each other. Where killing is not their first solution."

Asia, my old friend, sitting next to me on the bed, opened her bag. Behind the brush, behind the little folder that held her ID papers and passport, behind her thin wallet, she reached for a thicker, much more worn envelope that already sat open. It caught my eye. There were photographs in it. She sorted through them slowly, reverently, one by one, cooling her heart from the heat of discussion.

They were family pictures. In one, I could see part of Asia herself in a shiny dress, posing with others in a courtyard. It could have been a graduation photo. Another was a formal family shot; she looked younger in that one. All in all, there were about a half dozen photos. They had folds in them and were yellowed and ruffled at the edges. I guessed she touched them often.

"Abuk," Luel from across the room called me. "Now come over here. I'll do your hair next."

While I was gathering up my things, I saw Asia lingering with one photo more worn at the edges than any of them. It showed a bride and groom.

"Is that your wedding, Asia?"

She looked up, surprised to see me looking. "Yes. This is my husband."

"I heard he was here."

"He was here with me for about a month. Now he's at the front."

"It was good he was here."

"It was very good!" She held the photo like he was still here with her.

Mary called from across the room, "Oooh, you know the women are happy when their husbands come home!"

Another looked up from her braiding, "That's a honeymoon time!"

"And the husband goes back so soon, before they can be together long enough to have marriage troubles again!" The older women were laughing.

Luel interrupted, "And you know, this girl Abuk forgot to ask to have her husband here with her in the hotel!"

"She forgot?"

"I had to go and ask Riek Machar for her. She was toooo shy!"

But I protested, "I didn't forget!"

"Well, what then?"

"I didn't know! Dut and I just got here. After Maker settled us, he kissed us goodbye and went back to his room in the other place!"

"And you didn't say anything?"

"I thought it was a military rule."

Now they were really laughing at me.

"Abuk, you have to speak up!"

Mary, "So what did you do when you found that out, Luel?"

"I marched right up to Riek Macher and said, 'What do you think you are doing, bringing Abuk up here and leaving her husband outside?' Then he got ashamed and, I tell you, Maker was here in the D'Afrique that very night!"

When we got together we could shout and laugh and cry one after the other, with no silence in between. *This is a healing place.*

"Abuk, it's good you were in the camp."

"Why?"

"People know your father's family in Sudan."

"And people know Maker from the radio."

"It gives them courage to see people like us suffering with them in the camp."

This was Auntie Luel making this conclusion as her fingernails searched for hair to weave into a braid on my head. My hair was thin and broken off, nothing to braid.

So she created a braid out of air. This was her way to include me.

Karin was getting hungry, "Let's call room service and get some lunch up here. I need to eat."

"Ooh, Karin. It looks like you've been eating too well!" said the short woman across from me.

"Don't blame me! We are here six months and they feed us the best food and there is no work for us to do, no house to run."

I asked Karin, "Then in six months, I am going to look like you?"

They laughed and laughed, like they had all the time in the world.

Then Asia saw something, before I could pull my feet away.

"Abuk, what happened to your toes!"

My heart jumped, but I told her, "It's okay. They all used to be black underneath but now they're really better."

"But the nails are eaten up!" She grabbed one of my feet before I could hide it.

"It is no problem. It was the mud in Itang. It made my nails go bad."

"You should see a doctor."

"No, they're getting better."

"Not all of them."

Everyone was looking now at the two largest toes on my right foot. They were so ugly. So ugly. No one there had toes as ugly as mine.

"Then we'll just have to paint them!!" Asia announced.

Everyone agreed, "Put the brightest polish on her!"

"Who has the pink?"

"That will cure it!" And they were laughing again. And I was too.

Their hands were gentle and the polish felt cool as they covered my nail stubs with beautiful pink.

"All right, now you look like your mother's daughter!"

Auntie Luel was still working with what was left of my hair. She spoke to the others, "I heard something from my husband this week. There's trouble coming. The leaders met together here in Addis, five of the top commanders."

"What do you mean, trouble?"

"You know there's peace among us in this room, but there's fighting among the commanders."

"That shouldn't be."

"My husband was not there but he talks to a man who spends a lot of time around Garang."

"Who?"

"One of his drivers. He says the commanders don't trust each other. Not like we do. It matters to them who is from what tribe."

"They are always like this: Who is Dinka? Who is Nuer? Who is my brother?"

"Yes, and now even inside Dinka it matters to them if someone is Dinka Bor or Dinka Trige. And then Dinka and Nuer is a bigger problem."

"It's going to be a hard thing to take sides, if that's what they want to do. Dinka Bor and Dinka Trige people already got married and had children. And Dinka already married from Nuer and Nuer from Dinka. My grandmother on my father's side, she's Nuer. And my husband, his father was Nuer, but they moved to Dinka land and he married Dinka. So we are bound up in a two-tribe family."

"I heard that along the border, if the Nuer come and if a Dinka mother is there, they kill her."

"And that could bring a lot of pain between us now."

Some of the children, including Daniel and Dut, slipped back into our hotel room and fanned themselves out among the mothers and aunties. Little Daniel was the youngest son of Commander Kerubino. He was about the same size as Dut, but older. They were learning fast to be friends, but Daniel was fussy today.

Luel called to him, "Little Daniel, what do you want here?"

"I'm hungry, auntie."

"Come here to me!"

He smiled big and headed for Luel, who was holding out her arms, promising a hug as big and as wide as his arms were expecting. But their hug was interrupted.

"Daniel! Daniel! Where are you? All you kids get back here!" It was the loud voice of Shiloh, the young cousin who was watching the children. "Daniel! Get back in here!" She was all nerves with the responsibility her aunt had given her.

They were always warning the children to stay inside the rooms. The elevators in the halls were old and not safe. Sometimes a child would push his hand through the elevator door and have it cut when the elevator passed.

Daniel had charmed a cup of tea for himself from one of the women. At such a young age, he was as persuasive as his father. He left the room, running with the cup.

"You know, the men need to learn that it's better to talk than to fight."

"Because if you fight and you hurt someone, then it's too late, because hatred comes after that. And when hatred comes, the solution goes."

I thanked Luel for her weaving and got up and walked to the

window for some air. *How pretty this place is. How pretty they've made this part of the world.* From high up where we were, I could look down through streets around us and see the bright flowers that lined the paved walkways, the lush greenery that skirted our building, and the well-dressed people passing below. But I felt a little dizzy, so I stepped back. Heights were becoming a problem for me.

"Our families are mixed now. And friends are mixed too. I am Dinka Bor and here is Luel, Dinka Trige, standing behind me, braiding my hair!"

"And, Serah, you are Equatorian and I'm a Dinka Bor painting your toes!"

"But that driver heard Garang say you can only trust your own blood people."

"We are here raising our children together. Our husbands are spilling their blood together. How are we not one Sudanese?"

That's when we heard Shiloh scream. At first it didn't register with anyone. In Itang when you heard a scream, you were prepared for it, and you knew which way to run. But in the hotel, life was not like that. There was never screaming or loud weeping in the hotel or on the streets around it. Not by day or by night. Nobody expected to hear a scream in this place and nobody knew which way to run when they heard it.

Shiloh's screaming at first was from behind the walls that separated the two apartments. Then it quickly got louder, right next to us, outside in the hallway. By that time we were on our feet.

I cried out, too. "Dut! Dut, where are you!" *He is new here. He doesn't know the dangers. O God, not his hand!*

Just then I felt Dut pulling on my dress from behind as I turned toward the door to look for him. "Mama, Mama, why is she screaming?"

"Dut, honey!" I swept him up into my arms as I ran out the door with the others.

Now Shiloh was screaming, "Daniel fell down! He fell down!"

The women spread out. Asia ran down the hallway left, Lual right. Shiloh screamed louder, shaking and jumping.

"No, he fell from the window!" Then some turned and rushed into her room and to the window. Three or four of us rushed down the stairwell, thinking to catch him and stop his fall.

Hotel D'Afrique is an international hotel. The building is high. My room, where we were gathered, was 212, on the third floor. We ran down the stairwell, flying around the turns, helping each other keep upright, our voices echoing off the painted walls becoming a thousand voices as we ran.

But when we burst out of the doors into the courtyard, we burst into silence.

People were standing in a wide circle, frozen. No one moved. No one spoke. In the center of the blood-spattered courtyard, Daniel lay still, face down. We ran and knelt down and surrounded him.

The men had heard something too. They caught up with us in the courtyard and broke the silence.

"What is going on?" The people stared back at them without speaking.

"Does anybody know what happened?"

"Did anybody see the boy fall?" No one would answer.

After a time, a young European man came forward. His face was empty and pale. His hands were trembling.

"I thought it was a bundle of clothes falling. I thought about catching it, but then I thought, It's nothing." He was crying now, "So I stayed back." He pleaded with the men, "I didn't know! I didn't know!"

They rushed Daniel to the hospital, but he did not live. When we got there and found out there was no hope at all, even the men who were with us broke down. It is rare to see a Sudanese man cry. To them it is a sign of bravery to keep silent. But on that day even the men broke down and pulled together. If there was one thing they all could agree on it was a father's love for his son.

For days after that, the young girl who had watched Daniel fall did not speak. Her voice would not come out of her throat. The women were affected badly too. Our times together after this were not the same.

Things were happening everywhere that should not be happening anywhere. Death was in Itang. Death was here. Dut was not safe here either, because I did not know the dangers in this place like I knew them in the camp. As soon as we could, Maker and I moved with other families from there to safer hotel—a flat, sprawling complex with only one floor.

During our last night in the D'Afrique hotel, Maker and I lay awake in our bed. Sleep would not come.

"Abuk, since the time I left you in Itang, I was always thinking about you."

It was not usual for Maker to talk to me like this. The boy's death had opened his mouth.

"Since I left you, I was always thinking, if anything happened to you and Dut ...." He waited a minute to settle himself, "If anything happened to you, I know I couldn't live."

Dut was sleeping, so this was our time. He propped himself up on one arm so that I could see his face. "I missed you a lot."

"Maker, it was terrible for us there."

"I was so worried for you. At night I dreamed I couldn't find you anywhere."

I lay my head back and closed my eyes. I could not let myself feel his worries now. I was too tired.

"Since you are here, I am so happy." When I used to crowd around the radio in Itang hearing his voice, I imagined him here doing so well without me. Now the same voice was saying he needed me.

"I go to work happy now. Everybody sees it. They tell me, 'Maker, you are lucky to have her.'" He pulled me a little closer to him.

Three quarters of the women in Itang had their hearts broken by now. Many of the husbands, when they were a long time away, found other wives and never came back. But my husband had not done that.

"Abuk, I am lucky to have you."

I was too tired to hold two feelings in me anymore. I could not feel anger and love at the same time. So I let anger go.

11

GRANDDAUGHTER OF THE KING

The axe forgets but the tree remembers.

THE PAIN IN MY BELLY THAT HAD STARTED IN THE CAMP KEPT
growing in Addis. I was eating well now. The pain was in a different
place from my stomach, which had learned again to be satisfied and
at ease. But it didn't matter that now my days were safe and peaceful.
It didn't matter that now I had my husband saying he would protect
me. It didn't matter that I had forgiven him, and we were building our
family again. Nothing I did mattered. This pain in my belly would not
let go.

At the end of the first month, Maker arranged to send me to
England for help. His brother and his brother's wife would take me
in, I would go to a British hospital, and they would send me back to
Addis when I was well. That was his plan. But he also feared I would
decide to stay in England and apply for asylum there; he knew that I
could just disappear.

"Don't try it," he told me. But he feared even more that if I stayed
in Addis I would die.

Dut and I got off the plane at the London Heathrow Airport with
£900 sterling, my limited English, and passports that disguised our
family name. My husband was a well-known member of the SPLA

and I was also known. If certain people in England found out who we were, they might harm us. So I was frightened.

After we landed, I avoided the eyes of the customs officers as I walked along. But eventually one noticed me.

"Ma'am, where are you going?"

I stopped.

"Ma'am, where are you going? Do you have a place to stay in England?"

I looked over his shoulder to see if my brother-in-law was near. He was not.

"Ma'am, do you speak English?"

I understood him, but I did not want to answer.

"Do you speak Arabic?"

I nodded. He came back in a few minutes with a Sudanese man. This man spoke to me in Arabic.

"Where are you going, ma'am?"

"To my brother-in-law's house. My brother-in-law should be waiting outside for me."

"Are you one of John Garang's people?"

I tried to remember what it said on my passport. "No. I am from Ethiopia."

"You don't speak Arabic like an Ethiopian." He looked at me hard. "You speak like a Sudanese."

I said nothing more after that, so he and the customs officer examined my papers. The passport the SPLA had given me was for a diplomat. That was something the officer had to respect, but the Sudanese translator did not trust me.

I kept silent in front of them but there was no silence inside me. *Abuk, you are not a person good at telling lies. Are you a great diplomat? You can't even remember the name on your passport and you can't take it back to see. Who are you really? God help me.*

The customs officer and the translator walked with me wedged between them to baggage claim. There, I saw my brother-in-law waiting for me. I walked to him with dignity, like a diplomat might walk, holding back my raging instinct to run. I dared not greet him while the translator could hear me. On alert as well, my brother-in-law said only one thing to me in English, "Madame sister-in-law, welcome. I'll take you home." The officer and his translator did not take their eyes off us. I could feel their stare tracking us to the exit door.

Within a few days, my brother-in-law helped me get to his own doctor and then a specialist. They told me they had to do surgery immediately, even though my body was not strong enough. Something was growing in my belly, on my tubes.

There was no time to wait.

I did not wake up from surgery until the third day. When I awoke, the doctor spoke with me a little.

"Ms. Benjamin, I have been waiting for you."

I saw two identical doctors above me, then just one swaying with the walls and ceiling, then I saw two again.

"Ms. Benjamin, how are you?"

"I am okay." The clock on the wall was moving, too.

"How are you feeling?"

"I am okay."

"I have to say, you are a lucky woman...."

The £900 sterling that the SPLA sent for my living expenses, my brother-in-law used to pay for half the surgery. The rest he paid out of his own pocket, little by little, over time.

Time passed. When my sister-in-law invited me to go to market with her, I told her I could not. The last time I was here in London with them my first baby had died. It was the time when Princess Diana had her first son too, but her son did not die like mine did. It was a time of happiness for all in London, but not for me.

During my first stay, while I was watching my sister-in-law's twins in her London apartment, a strong explosion nearby shook everything. On the TV they said that two IRA bombs had blown up and killed a dozen soldiers and horses and injured many other people in the park close by. Then two hours later, while we were still huddled by the TV, I felt the hard hit of another bomb, and I knew that people were being hurt and killed all around me. That was 1982; now, in 1986, whenever my sister-in-law asked me to go out, I relived that day and said, "No thank you, sister. I am tired."

So my sister-in-law went shopping for me herself. She bought me dresses in size twelve because she wanted me to be myself again, but they didn't fit. I was still not even size two.

They also sent me to English class in the evenings. This was something I wanted so much that I went out of the house for it. English was a language that could help me and my son survive anywhere.

One night, my brother-in-law sat with me to talk. "Abuk, you can stay here in England as long as you want. We can help you get an apartment here and a job, if that's what you would like."

Maker had warned me that they would offer me this. "Abuk, what do you say? You can obtain asylum."

Do not ask me to do this. I promised I would not.

"Africa is too dangerous now."

And England is not?

"I will talk to your husband. Please consider staying."

Maker's brother was a modern man. He could not fathom why a woman believed she had to stay, or even die, beside her husband. But we knew back home that the men who had no wives nearby them died in greater numbers at the front, for lack of food, for lack of love.

"I will think about this," I told him. But I was only thinking about how to tell him no.

Dut and I returned to Addis Ababa in early 1987. When I left Addis a year before, my hands were empty. When I returned now, I brought bags full of the things my sister-in-law had bought. When I got back, I sent them to my sisters in Itang.

They had a much greater need of these things.

But when I got back to Addis I found Maker distracted again, busy with the war. On my return though, too, I also found my high school friend, Anip. She was younger than me and very smart. Her husband she had loved from the very first day she saw him. But, unlike mine, hers allowed her to delay their marriage until after her graduation.

She was always a restless, forceful girl. Anger and fun and love had always beat their wings in her like three birds tied together. Her husband was like her, too, a young commander in the SPLA in Addis, like my husband. The two men, intellectuals both, often talked into the night, worried for the direction of the war. Our two families were close then.

In August, six months after I was back from England, she told me, "Abuk, I am pregnant!"

"Anip, I am too, but no one knows it yet."

"Well, I am going to tell everyone. It is a great thing to bring a child into the world." This was going to be her first, so she was abandoned to her excitement.

"It is hard to raise a child in a foreign land, Anip. Very hard." She had not been to Itang. And I had not told her much.

"Foreign land?" She would hear none of it. "We have each other!"

Very soon the news spread, and everyone was applauding our husbands' good fortune.

Then one day in September, Anip heard a loud knock on her apartment door. "Where is your husband?" SPLA guards filled the doorway.

"He is resting in our bedroom."

"Wake him. He's coming with us."

"To the war again? So soon?"

"No, to prison."

"To prison! Why?"

"He's a traitor. Wake him, if he's really sleeping."

She refused but they overtook her, broke through the bedroom door, dragged her husband out by the collar.

"What do you think you are doing?" He fought to push them off.

"You are guilty of treason." They wrestled him down.

"I will tell Garang. He will have you shot!"

"Good luck. It is Garang who sent us!"

They took him while Anip screamed and beat them with her fists. They took him to God knows where, and she never heard from him again. That's when her health turned bad and the baby in her tried to come out. There was no place on earth for either of them but the hospital.

Maker, more careful now, had been so glad to see me. He had gotten me pregnant too soon after my surgery and now with the shock of this arrest I was in trouble, bleeding before my time. Anip and I were both admitted to the Zewditu Hospital in Addis Ababa within days of each other. I hoped at least to room with her there. But things did not go as I'd planned.

When the medical assistant wheeled me into my room, a woman my mother's age lay still on the other bed. By her, a female guard sat straight, her right hand on the gun across her lap, staring at me and at the attendant as I inched from my wheelchair to the bed. The older woman stared too, studying me.

Hers was the last face I saw because I was weak and quickly drifted to a dreaming place. There, human forms and languages moved across my mind. English marched by, while German words shot across my sky like bullets; I felt my brain awash in French and the flowing Ethiopian language of kings. Male and female voices, trembling, rumbling, whispering, going, coming, shoe against floor chafing, until suddenly at various, unmeasured intervals a female soldier's bark commanded me and all the people in my dreams to silence.

When I finally opened my eyes to my husband's voice, he told me it was my second day in hospital.

He had brought a basket with contents wrapped in cloth. "Abuk, I have something for you." Six boiled eggs lay nested inside.

"Maker, who made these?"

"I did," he said low, looking around. "Eat and get well." This was the first time in all our life together he had prepared food for me.

He placed the basket on my bedstand. "Dut is asking for you," he said.

"How is he?"

"Fine."

"Who is feeding him?"

Maker's younger brother, standing by unnoticed until now,

answered, "My wife keeps him with our other children." Maker's father had many wives so Maker had many brothers. This was a brother I had not yet met.

"I would keep him with me, Abuk, but we are overwhelmed at the radio station now."

"What's happening?"

"There is trouble coming."

"What is coming?"

"I cannot tell you."

Maker and his brother prepared to leave.

"Will you come tomorrow?"

"If I can." He bent down whispering in Dinka, "Say, who is that woman?" He nodded toward the other bed. "She has many guests."

"What guests?"

"You have not noticed?"

I've only dreamed.

"People from many places in the world. Is she a government minister?"

"I don't know."

"You haven't talked to her?"

"No. I don't even remember why I am here."

He pulled out his glasses and cleaned them, like he did when he studied his speeches and his books. "Two days ago you were cramping and weak, vomiting, fainting. You don't remember? The doctor feared you might lose the baby."

Then I remembered the crush of bodies close around me, the weight of my own body being carried out into a crowded street, my hand on the strap above the window as our car leaned into turns. "And the baby?"

"You carry the baby still." Thanks rose from my heart to my eyes and overflowed.

Maker told me to rest, that he would be back. He shifted his eyes to a dark-skinned man standing by the older woman's bed. A suit, well-made but worn, hung loosely on the man's lean frame. He and the woman spoke in German while the native guard stared at the floor, tilting her head when either the man or the woman moved. She looked up briefly when my husband left the room.

The walls of this small room were a dull tan scrubbed lifeless. On the floor, white rays of afternoon sun highlighted a web of scars—deep, historic carvings made by, I imagined, graveled shoes, ragged table legs, and mops worn down to metal. The stench of stomach sickness, sweat, and antiseptic soap spread rumors of unfolding grief from up and down the hall.

I rose slowly to find a bathroom. The guard shifted. Our window faced the afternoon sun, under whose glare the view that stretched out below would have been entirely bleached, but for the fact that someone had hung curtains. Gauzy, bright, and breathy curtains, made of threads spun from the colors of a happier time. They overlaid the streets with shimmering pastel petals, leaves, and drifting feathers; they gave radiance to the dusty breeze.

My walk to the bathroom was long and slow, though just across the room. The trip back was even longer, more unsteady. I pushed the egg basket back from the edge of the bed stand and lay back, working my spine into a trough between the mattress lumps, and spread my hands like grape leaves over the child now sleeping inside me.

Early, early, the next morning, drops of water on my face entered my dreams then quickly drew me from them. I guessed that it was 4 or 5 a.m. A low song of male voices roused my ear. I saw bearded, dark-robed men sway gently around the woman's bed. Another stood not two feet away from me, a branch of dewy hyssop raised above me, a halo of light around it. Then sleep drew me back in.

"Good morning," the woman said. By now the room was full of daylight. "I'm sorry. Did they wake you?" She spoke in English. "I asked them to bless you, too."

English was neither my first nor second language but with effort I could understand enough and, with more effort, speak.

"The guard is on break." She said, again in English.

Her eyes were eager as her thin frame turned to face me. "I am Sofia." She spoke softly. "Your name?"

"Abuk Jervas Makuac."

"Do you know why they put you here with me?"

"No."

"You are not Ethiopian and cannot speak Amharic. They think you won't try to help me."

"Who are you?"

"Granddaughter of King Haile Selassie."

As I listened, I thought of my own grandfather too.

"Twelve years ago, men betrayed and killed my grandfather the king. Did you hear about it?" She searched my eyes for understanding.

"I'm sorry. I was just a girl."

"They killed my brother." She slowed down now, making sure I could understand her words. "My mother...myself...my three sisters...have been in prison since then...." Her words spread out, like blood seeping slowly from a wound. "My grandfather...the king...was murdered...killed...in the first year."

"I'm sorry." I felt ashamed that I didn't know and that I didn't know enough words in English to comfort her.

"I became too sick in prison; they had to bring me here."

"The guard is to protect you then?" I asked.

"No."

The door latch stirred, and we stopped. When the guard strode in, she saw nothing more than her hated prisoner, lying on her side, and a pregnant Sudanese girl asleep on the other bed.

Our friendship grew.

"The guard goes out at about this time each day, before the time of visitors." It was morning again. A full day had passed. Maker had not returned.

The woman's voice had music in it, a music that one feels through other sounds, a music that fills gaps in conversation. "Look out the window," she said, "across the river that runs below. See? There, the building my grandfather built. Red Lion Hospital."

All the buildings looked alike to me.

"If my grandfather were still king," she said, "I would have you there with me, with the best doctors in charge."

Our door swung open and the female guard strode in, agitated, followed by women bearing gifts arranged in open baskets. They laid flat bread and a variety of cheeses on the woman's bedstand.

My roommate whispered in English between her teeth, her head turned away from me. "These are old friends. They have been waiting years to see me."

Every morning, when we were alone again, she offered me a part of whatever her foreign friends had brought her, especially the oranges and cheese. She found out I liked these things very much. In addition to my gratitude, she earned my respect.

"That first terrifying night in prison," she said, "I never thought I would see the light of day again." She ran her hand over her graying, thinning hair. "They shaved our heads, even my blessed mother's, and threw us into a deep hole, a place that we shared with rats." She rubbed her hands and arms. I wondered how many bite marks there had been.

"In the camp I feared rats, too." I told her. "I was sick with worry for my son. I felt so...."

"...helpless." Her voice was knowing, regal, calm. "I worried for my mother, too. The lice would not leave her; her cough would not clear. The guards did not hear me at all when I called them. Some days..."

"...you hated them." I said, showing that I understood too. *Our feelings are the same.*

Sofia stopped the conversation. I thought she feared the guard would soon be back, with her gun and her unhappy looks. But she went on in a softer voice, "A prophet once said, 'Only love is the way out of prison.'"

Her large eyes, dark and deep, called to mine. Her face, gaunt and subtly aged, did not have the bitter lines so commonly cut deep by years of rage.

"I tell you, when you forgive the ones who hate you, they leave your heart, and you leave theirs." She raised her eyes like one who looks out on a flowering field.

"But if they still hate you?" I asked.

She shook her head and said no more.

Very early the next morning, after the night guard had gone and before the next one could arrive, two soldiers I'd never seen before came quickly, bringing an older and a younger woman. "Eh-my-eh! [Mother!]," Sofia whispered to the older one and *"Eh-heht! Tanash heht!* [Little sister!]" to the younger. They embraced, wept. Then in the next breath, the soldiers asked forgiveness and took them out before the daily guard came.

Sofia cupped water in both hands then and washed her face. "A few of the soldiers still love us." She wiped her face and her tears on the small hospital towel.

When the day came for her discharge and her own return to jail, I was not ready. I still had questions. At her last step through the door, she looked back, her back straight, head up, and smiled to me. What did it feel like to have so much love while being betrayed by one's own people? I did not know at the time that soon I myself would have a chance to find out.

"THERE IS AN IMPORTANT MEETING IN THE CITY TONIGHT," MAKER said during his first visit in many days. His high forehead glowed darkly under the glare of the ceiling bulb. "So I must go now." He folded and refolded his glasses and tried again to slide them into his shirt pocket. He steadied himself against the rusting bed frame.

The truth was that I was pregnant and still in the hospital and felt less interesting to my husband. "It is the fourth month, Maker. The child moves." I slid my hand across my growing belly and looked into his face.

During his absences, I could imagine him responding, but in his presence I could not.

"I must go," he said again, stiffening, distracted.

When he did not visit, the days were longer but there were also fewer times when my mind went darting like an angry hen hunting some other explanation for the sour sweetness on his breath, the glassy vacancy in his eyes.

"Will you visit again soon?" I asked.

"Soon."

Soon was starting to be seldom. Then after the longest absence, one day he told me, "Changes are coming. I'm going to the warfront."

"What kind of changes?"

He looked away. "Dut will continue to stay with my brother. You will stay on in the hospital until the baby is born." His tone was flat and final. "The SPLA office will decide for you from there."

And that was it. Before my baby was born, before I was better, before a name for a boy or a girl had been chosen, Maker left Addis for the warfront with his friends, the commanders.

By early 1987 I had healed enough to be discharged from the hospital. So now I was alone again, in a strange city, with only one close friend. We were left to face the hardships of both war and pregnancy alone. On April 27, 1987, my first daughter, Aker, was born in the Zewditu Hospital. I was lucky—so lucky—that I did not give birth to her in the camp. SPLA had wanted to send me back to Itang toward the end of my pregnancy. But even though I had been discharged, I kept having fevers and bleeding, so every month they would give me permission to stay a little bit longer.

Between trips to the hospital, I was permitted to stay in the SPLA hotel. But in the second trimester of my pregnancy, I had to move out. They needed the room for an SPLA officer. I spent two months after that in the household of John Garang, until finally my daughter and I were placed in the house of a local woman. Her house was small, and its walls were cracked. You could see through them and watch the people outside walking by.

Then, when Aker was three months old, an officer spoke to me. "The SPLA cannot pay your upkeep here in the city anymore," he said. "You are well. You will go back to Itang on the next transport out."

My heart stopped. But its condition was not noted nor cared for.

1 2

OLDER AND WISER

Sticks in a bundle are unbreakable.

THE TRIP FROM ADDIS TO ITANG WAS DIFFERENT THIS TIME. THE FIRST time I traveled this road, it stretched on before me with wonder, swelled in front of me with hope and the heady thrill of a new cause, an unknown destination, and the promise of a new home in a safer land. The road is plainer now. Once lined with my dreams and memories of tree-trimmed streets and well-fed, well-wishing friends, it is today no more than the dusty road it always was. Crude mountains lined it and walled us in, then broke to sudden cliffs threatening to throw us to the wind. *Oh driver, please slow down!* I rocked my son and infant daughter with the rocking of the van.

Their decision was that Maker and I would meet again in Gambela, our last stop some years ago before arriving at Itang. It was a common meeting place where two national roads funneled down together, one from Addis Ababa on the east and the other from the Sudanese border on the west, there joining irreversibly and emptying out into the camp at Itang.

MAKER CAME BY TRUCK ON THE WEST ROAD FROM THE BATTLEFRONT at Maban. The children and I arrived from Addis on the east road and set out to find him in town. I pulled Dut and my suitcase with one hand and held Aker on my hip. I was walking on feet now swollen from bracing against the van those long hours through the mountains.

"Abuk, over here!" Maker called out from a gathering of men in the open market. He stood uniformed and alert, engaged in agitated discussion with the other men. He motioned for us to join them.

I had passed my time in Addis sick, pregnant, nursing. I was still thin. When he squeezed the three of us together in his arms, we were like bundles of tall grass bound up for the fire.

"Comrades, this is my little girl! Look at her!" He held up Aker, "How old is she?"

"Three months."

"Three months!" He turned to rebuke me in front of them. "You brought her here now, so small? It will be rainy season and to travel she must be at least six months!"

"The office sent us."

"Why didn't you tell them her age?"

"I told them."

Maker invited one of the men to walk with us through Gambela's market.

This town was not a big place; it had one or two small hotels, inexpensive, mildewed. The town's buildings were intermixed with huts. At the crossroads of the floodplain, it had become a singular trading place. Cattle moved slowly here and there on the streets. But the market was good and if I had had money—oh, if I'd had money to spare—I would have bought some of the things traded here from far.

"Abuk, this is Mabior. We fought side by side at the front," Maker took my arm to hold my attention as we walked. Mabior looked straight ahead, silent.

I was distracted, looking through every stall for a bowl like the bowls we have in Sudan. Our bowls are round and broad. On them we unfold a great circle of brown *injera* bread, smoothing it thin and soft, draping it like a cloth over the basket's wide edge. On *injera* we place fresh stew of fragrant beans, sharp cheese, and slow-cooked meat and greens.

"At the front we lived one day to the next. Bombs came too often." His pace quickened.

The virtue of our kind of basket is it brings people together. Each person in the family and each guest pull a piece of the broad flat bread and roll for themselves a mouthful of *injera* and stew, and then pull again and roll another mouthful.

"The crush of battle is something you have never felt, Abuk." Maker stopped and looked to his friend for confirmation then fixed his eyes on mine. "Every minute was a matter of life and death, but we survived."

Around the Sudanese basket we eat together until the blanket of bread, the filling of stew, the pleasure of loving company has been fully savored and swallowed down and there is no more hunger and no more tears.

His back straightened. "You have never felt anything as terrible as this!" He turned to walk on with Mabior.

But there were none of these baskets here today. The baskets on the stands today were long and narrow, sand colored, striped with dark brown. The Gambela people use them not for eating but for tossing grains into the air to break the outer shell. Afterwards, the naked grains lie on top to be taken. The husks are poured out on the ground and the breeze takes them away.

"Markhur, my close friend, do you remember him?" Maker stopped again. "He was killed this week beside me."

I knew Markhur, too, and I felt the loss in my heart. "He was a good man," I said. But I thought, I knew so many good women in the camp, too, who also died afraid and for nothing.

I do not dare to spend my money at this market. Hunger waits for us in Itang. With such little food, how will I make enough milk to nurse my baby? Asthma waits for Dut. Malaria waits for me. There has always been too little quinine.

"But of course she does not understand. She is just a woman." He said to Mabior as he reached to take my arm. But I shifted Aker to my left side where he stood, and held Dut's hand on the right.

Where the man goes, our tradition says the wife must go or she is no wife. And where the wife is, children are and more children come and then hunger and danger grow. You may shoot your gun once and kill your enemy. But there is no trigger you can pull just once to stop our hunger.

He turned to speak to me again. "I will take you back to Itang and I will meet with the men there, and then return to fighting."

Throughout the market, tethered goats chafed, ears and tails up, pulling at their ropes. Big bells rang around their necks, advertising their use in breeding, barter, slaughter.

"Abuk, the truck is leaving. Get on with the children. I will go with the men in the jeep."

We met up again at the camp on the second day of rain. Not far from the main road was my own hut, which I had left in the care of Ngor, an old man. He had agreed to keep it up for me until I returned.

"Uncle Ngor, how are you?"

He emerged from the hut, stooped and staggering.

"Are you well, uncle?"

The hut was cracked in many places, the grasses of the roof were thinned out and separated.

"Sister...."

I know how much time and strength it takes to go for the best mud to repair cracks in the walls. I know how much money it takes to buy new grass for a roof.

"Sister, and Brother Maker. Welcome...."

It takes the same amount of money to buy beer.

The man appeared embarrassed.

"Uncle, you have kept the hut well," my husband said.

A hut with this many cracks welcomes rats, then snakes will follow soon to eat the rats. The rains will most likely open up what's left of the roof this season. Maker and I looked at each other. I shook my head. This was beyond repair.

Maker spoke, "Uncle, for your kindness we thank you greatly." The man bowed. "Uncle, you may keep this hut."

Uncle Ngor's mouth dropped. "But...."

"You have earned it," Maker told him. The old man's shoulders loosened up, relieved.

"God bless you both," he said as he turned to go back and lie down and drink more under the leaking roof.

Maker said to me, "Habsa's place is not far. She and her husband will take us in."

Her husband, Malual, was a teacher in the camp, a man of peace. He and Maker often disagreed, but in the rains, one puts one's differences aside. Anyway, they had little chance this time for discussion. Maker would leave in a few days. Habsa and Malual, as hoped, welcomed us, and invited my children and me to stay on.

In the time that followed, from the shelter of my good friend's hut, my little son and I reacquainted our hearts with camp. I was so glad to have Habsa by my side to make my return easier. Old friends came by to surprise us.

"Asunta!" I leaped to see her.

"Abuk, come here and let me hug you!" How I missed her loud voice and big arms, though thinner now, still strong. "How are you? How is Dut? Where is Maker?" Asunta could never ask just one thing.

Other women and their children came with her to greet me and my suddenly very happy boy. From every side their questions came at me.

"Have you seen my cousin Christine?"

"Are the men still training in Addis?"

"A boy came here from my village, lost. Have you heard about an attack on Bir Di?"

"I am sorry, so sorry," I told them. "I bring no news. But come, see what I did bring."

At the door of Habsa's hut and on the stones in front, I spread out my gifts. The women leaped and chattered. They passed the shimmering clothes from hand to hand and held them up to themselves and to each other. As they carried on, I invited a certain one of them into the hut.

"Achai, take this." Achai had told me once how she could endure anything in camp except tying menstrual rags with wire to her waist.

That shame affected her more badly than it affected any of us each month.

When she peeled back the wrapping to see two boxes of sanitary pads, her hands tightened and her eyes closed.

"Thank you, Abuk. Thank you. Thank you." Her tears flowed.

"Achai, you are too sensitive," I said, laughing, and brought her back with me out to the sun.

After this I also had my dark reunion with the daily fight to live as I rejoined the women in our cooking circle to draw water from the river, boil it, strain it, trade things for scraps of food, grind hard grain, gather what wood we could find to keep our fires going.

Every third morning the duty to go for water fell to Asunta and me. This was no small matter, for water brought both life and death. Eggs of insidious worms, bones of the sudden dead, dark leakings from latrines all floated in camp water. It was our task to make it drinkable. We who knew each other did this work together and trusted no one else.

This day, we had reached the tall grasses, and it was time to fill the great *jerkanas* (our word for the flat-sided jerry cans) with water. We selected the place where the water flowed and refreshed itself a little.

"Good enough," Asunta said. We pushed the *jerkanas* down till murky water filled them. "Let's pull them through the grass before we carry them. I will not put these dirty things on my clean head!"

"City girl!" I chided her.

Our wading in and out of the river disturbed a stand of great white egrets. First one, then all spread broad, angelic wings. Bright white and pure and thickly feathered, they pulled themselves into the air. *Where in all this mud do they get such whiteness for their wings? How do these angels breed themselves so perfectly in hell?*

"Have your children gotten infections from this water, Asunta?"

"No."

Two dragonflies swirled above the river, too, one sparking purple and the other, sweet orange. *Where in this drabness do they get their colors?*

"It's because I rub my children's legs with oil," she said.

This may be a sin, I think, of city women. We used the UN cooking oil to shine our skin and rub our children down, too. Because of it, how easily we could wash this mud right off them every night. With oil, their skin was smooth; no little crack could open on their legs to let in worms.

In the corner of my eye, I caught movement at the newly filled-up warehouse down the road. The flood waters had relented some this week, and just yesterday UN trucks had come through to deliver goods. Now we were waiting for their distribution.

"I never carried water this way in my life." Asunta put down her jug and rubbed her head. "And I think the sun is turning my black skin blacker!" She looked down and stroked her long, thin arms with much affection.

Military trucks, like the one that brought us here the first time, were backing up to the food storage.

"Asunta, what are they doing?" Uniformed men jumped down and hauled heavy bags out. Bag after bag, they threw into their trucks.

"Army trucks follow UN trucks like jackals follow deer." Asunta helped me lift the water jug back onto my head. "You didn't know that?"

The growl of engines deepened now as the trucks swerved heavily away.

"There you go! Less food for us!" she said and clapped her hands.

On the days I have no food to eat, I have no strength to break out of sadness, the sadness of hearing children cry, the sadness of worry when people die. It is this sadness that makes us prisoners of war.

"Come on, Abuk. Let them go! There's nothing we can do!" she said.

Just as the sun broke to its full light in the morning sky, we arrived back at our compound carrying our *jerkanas* full of churned-up river water. We prepared the purifying fire and pulled the empty boiling pots near.

Later, the rain put out our fire, as it often did. So we boiled our water and cooked what food we had inside. In the rainy season, the damp smoke inside our huts choked our lungs and burned our eyes. It was this way for so many days, I did not try to count them.

One morning when the clouds cleared, a small, barrel-chested man walked into our compound. He wore an old suit jacket, out of place in our world of mud. He carried his shoes and had his pant legs rolled up. Asunta and Habsa knew him.

"Father Benjamin! How are you?" they said.

"I am strong, sisters. And how are you?"

"Fine. We are all well."

"Praise God."

"You have not been here for many days."

"I have been visiting the leaders. But they won't hear me."

Asunta spread a place for him on the high ground under our large tree. He leaned back and stretched his legs, but his breath did not easily catch up with him.

"You know our history," a gurgling cough broke up his words, "how the British…" he cleared his throat, "…took over all Sudan."

Habsa brought him a cup of weak tea.

"Thank you, sister." His breath was raspy, his voice a mournful wheeze. "And Christian missionaries came in after them, and we accepted them."

She filled his cup again.

"And where is the West now? They turn their backs on us! So who are my Sudanese brothers turning to for help?"

Habsa looked at me and tilted her head toward our cooking fire. There was grain there and a little goat meat simmering for the children.

"They turn to the communists, who will give them guns."

She poured clean water into a basin, brought it and knelt beside him.

He dipped his hands.

"But to get the communists' help, they have to accept their books. And their books insist there is no God at all."

He wet his face and wiped it with a graying cloth he carried with him for that purpose.

"This is a great dilemma. With their mouths our commanders denounce God, but secretly they come to me and ask for prayer. It is an intolerable hypocrisy!"

I set before him a tin of cooked grain and in it the shred of meat we had boiled to share among three families.

"Their hearts and minds are conflicted over this. And I tell them, when a leader's own heart rebels against him—his army will too."

He breathed heavily and ate eagerly, like there was no one else in the world.

"I am here as someone who stands up and says, 'There is God,' and the people in this camp believe me."

He dipped his hands in the water basin a second time and wiped his mouth and put into his jacket pockets the boiled dough that Habsa had given him.

"I thank you for your Christian hospitality, my sisters. The leaders may reject God, but the people here have not. God bless you." He stood up and stepped back into the standing water with the faith that brought him and walked on, his pants rolled up, his pockets full, his shoes under his arm.

IN THE FIRST YEARS, SO MANY CHILDREN DIED FROM DIARRHEA AND other illnesses. After running to the UN hospital again and again, we began to learn the medicines and other remedies. To stop the diarrhea, we learned to mix salt, lemon and boiled water. The lemons we bought from our sources outside the camp. Once we learned the names of other medicines, we traded for them in Gambela and stock-piled them in our huts. Then whenever we heard of someone sick, we ran with the medicine to their hut and helped them heal. We women prevented many deaths in the camp after we learned these things. No one had to run the long way to the hospital anymore. We brought the medicine to them. This was how we showed our love.

In those difficult days, whenever we saw a passenger plane flying high overhead, we said, "Oh, those people are happy. But look at us here. When those people look down, they just see little spots of light from our fires. Do they have any idea what kind of people are down here and what we are suffering?"

There was an old woman called Mama Geer, who came to me one day with oil from the seed of a green sweet fruit grown mainly in my hometown Rumbeck, and with it honey, shea oil, and shea fruit. She was a healer woman and had heard that my son was ill with breathing sickness. She taught me how to mix and cook the medicine, make him drink it, and put it in his nose. After she treated him, he coughed up all the green sickness in him and started to be okay. So I kept this recipe and the rest of the ingredients with me in my hut for others.

Our friend Mary was in charge of our section of the camp, Telon 5, with two thousand people in it. She appointed seven leaders. The leaders went from hut to hut to learn how much rice, how much corn, how much oil each household needed. When food came, the leading women distributed it according to the count. After a time there was also an older woman put in charge of medicine. If a household had sickness and needed medication, they applied to her. Then she would go to Gambela to trade some of their oil, rice, and corn for the medicine they needed, some for now and some to store in their huts for the future.

But that was not the only service Mary coordinated. On a regular schedule, fifteen women from among us would walk six hours to a secret place outside the camp. Some would carry sugar, rice, and cooking oil, and the old woman would take some of our medicines. They would leave at sunrise and get to that place at noon to feed and tend to the wounded SPLA soldiers. This had to be done quietly and at a distance from the camp because the UN could not know.

Mary and I were also assigned as wedding planners. We took the role of aunts to the bride and groom. We borrowed dresses for the bride from newly arrived refugees. But our tradition also made things more difficult. If the wedding happened in the rainy season we had to keep the bride's feet untouched by mud. And because no man was allowed to touch anything that touched the bride on her wedding day, we women had to carry the bride in a chair to her destination. But one of the brides, she was too big for us to keep her out of the mud, so we had to call the men. This happened only once.

It was also a tradition among us that if a woman had teenage daughters, we mothers would give some of our food to the girls also, so that they would be fatter and the boys would want them for marrying.

Eventually we got a UN prize for Telon 5. The UN staff said they had never seen a camp so clean as ours and even with furnishings. They asked, "Where did you get these things?" We told them we went to the forest, cut wood and built the things ourselves. It was better not to tell them about our lively trade, especially our sale of UN supplies. We had strong and fair leadership in those days and wanted nothing to disturb it. Nuer, Dinka, Equatorial, and others, women from every tribe. Mary organized our section that way with a hidden purpose, to make sure the leading women from all the tribes would have to work as one to survive.

13
BETRAYAL

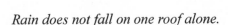

Rain does not fall on one roof alone.

BEFORE AKER TURNED ONE YEAR OLD, MAKER HEARD THAT BOTH HIS children had been suffering breathing sickness. Word got to him that there was a time when I had rushed them one after the other gasping for air to the camp hospital for injections. It was true. I had. Then word got to me he was on his way.

During the time I was in Malual and Habsa's compound, while Maker was still at the front, I had set myself to build a hut of my own as I had before. I was more experienced this time, and there was more cooperation, but time and material shortage required this hut to be smaller than my former one. So I added a small food storage and cooking place close by.

It was into the new hut that Maker suddenly appeared one day.

"Why aren't you taking better care of my children?" were his first words.

"I am!" *Where have you been? You have not sent us any help.*

"You are a lazy woman, talking all day with your friends!" *You are a useless man. The husbands of my friends have either stayed or sent help.*

Dut crept up behind me and leaned his head into the back of my neck. "Mama," he whispered. "Papa's back. Why is he mad at you?"

"What? You don't answer me?" Dut ducked his head and dug his fingers into my ribs. "And every woman in this camp takes a lover when her husband is gone!"

He raised his hand. "You are no different." I felt Dut's shoulders draw up, his small body starting to throb. "Because of you my children are sick!" Dut held his coughing in.

It is because of you that they are even here, man. I raised my arm up to defend myself. *Why didn't you send us to a good place like you promised? Why did you lie to me at the airport?*

"And where is my food? You knew I was coming." Will new bruises rise now on my arms, already hurting from pounding out the grain, will they hurt now too from the pounding of your anger? *How stupid I was to be loyal and come back to you.*

"At least I hoped my wife would give me a meal!" *I have sold everything anyone who ever loved me gave to me to feed these children. What food do you deserve?*

I was surprised when he suddenly dropped back onto the clay bench, breathing heavily, sitting himself up on his two hands—his arms sinewy, their veins ribboning out and twisting. "You are no wife!"

"I have been faithful!" *I have been foolish.* I sat down on the floor and pulled Dut onto my lap. Did Maker even see him?

"You have failed me!" he said. But I saw that there was no water in his mouth to even spit, and his sound was weakening.

We sat in stillness for a long time, Maker working to calm his breath, I leaning my head back against the wall, stroking Dut's head as he calmed himself, too, all of us listening to an unusual silence outside. No doubt, Habsa had heard our fight and had put my baby to sleep inside her hut. I was sure that everyone in the circle had heard.

THE RHYTHM OF CAMP LIFE RESUMED AS THE UN FOOD disbursements came again. Maker stayed all day with the men who listened to news on the radio and discussed the future of the war with one another. But there was peace again between Maker and me, the peace of silence and defeat.

One night, as Maker and I lay in the hut's dampness, children asleep, our stomachs pained but still, men appeared outside the hut door.

"Maker Benjamin?"

My husband rose. "I am here."

"Come out."

The air outside was full of muted human voice and movement. Next to my head I heard the hiss of rough cloth sliding up past rough thighs. Then I saw Maker's suddenly uniformed frame pass quickly through the hut door, haloed by the moon.

Their voices met his.

He returned, urgent. "Abuk, there is great trouble at the front. I must leave tonight." He packed some things quickly. Half out the door again, he looked back and said, "Take better care of my children."

The scrape and crush of booted feet, the throaty smack of long guns thumping rhythmically against men's backs, promised a new advance, signaling that Maker would be at the front again for many days. On our narrow bed I now rolled on my back, breathed deep, stretched out my sore limbs, their knots untying slowly with my thoughts.

When the next day broke, there was much stir in the camp.

"John Garang has found treason in the movement!"

"Many men were arrested last night!"

But in our small compound there was order still, and duty, and normal tasks to do.

"Habsa, Maker was called to the front again last night," I confided to my closest friend.

She looked sad. "I am so sorry, Abuk," she said.

Then the day turned worse. Mayan, whom I had known from Wau, came running up to me with news.

"My husband was arrested last night!" She was sobbing.

"Something strange is happening." I tried to comfort her, "My husband is gone too. He was called away to the front last night."

"That's what they told mine," she answered. "They told him they needed him. But now I heard that they came to arrest him." She collapsed against my hut door.

"Mayan, where did you get this news?"

"It is all through the camp. They have accused your husband of treason, too."

"No, I don't believe you!"

She turned away; she knew her news and her alarm were both unwelcome. Unwelcome.

The night that followed this was long. My eyes opened with every noise, hoping to see my husband stooping, reentering our hut. But only empty moonlight entered, pointing out the doorway's gaping loneliness. And when I closed my eyes to sleep, I found that sleep had left me too. Out the same door.

The arrests did not stop with the first sweep. The mornings of many of the next days were jarred by cries of other women whose husbands or sons were taken. Our days were darkened too by the long shadows of soldiers. Men who had been living among us and had blended in, were suddenly uniformed, edgy. In the daylight they did not show their guns but their eyes and presence were enough. Even after those first weeks, when their uniforms were exchanged again for rags, their eyes still darted everywhere.

"Mommy, where is Auntie Habsa? Why don't you talk to her anymore?"

"She doesn't talk to me, Dut."

"The soldiers made her afraid, but they're gone now, Mama."

"They're not gone. You just don't see them."

"Why didn't they take Uncle Malual too?" I watch Habsa duck into her hut bearing a bowl of steaming grain and a tin of boiled tea water.

"I don't know, Dut."

"He still lets me come into their hut to play."

"He is a good man."

"But he does not come out to play with us anymore."

"He is a smart man." Habsa emerged with male and female laundry for the day. She gathered up her child and with her basket walked alone toward the river, her eyes fixed on the path. In those days it was the pride of a woman to have a man's laundry to wash.

"And why don't Auntie Yom and Auntie Asunta talk to you anymore?"

"Dut, please, no more questions."

The soldiers had branded me a traitor's wife. The walk to the river for water alone now was very long. The cooking fire I kept lit for myself alone. My isolation was one long, speechless day, lived over and over again—a one-woman, dark eternity.

After sunset, I would lie down to ache and argue with the night. I would close my eyes to block out emptiness and bring up better memories to soothe the pain. I imagined the warm cooking fire in Habsa's compound. On my eyelids I watched Asunta, Yom, and Habsa moving freely, stirring the boiling grain, feeding the fire one crackling stick at a time, talking and working as the children played among them. I dreamed men brought their radio near and listened until it was time to share the last food scraps of the day, as the low, metallic voice of garbled good and bad news, the at once acrid and sweet smell of burning wood and cooking grains mixed themselves with the bitter sweetness of my own soul. In my dreaming mind I drifted hungry for assurance into their circle but my dreams betrayed me, too. In them I saw Asunta's back turn, I saw the sad side of Habsa's face as she looked down. Even in my dreams Yom and the other women all walked away. The men turned off the radio. Then I would open my eyes to shed my tears.

I am no traitor! Why do they treat me as a traitor? They have betrayed me! They are the traitors—all of them!

Dut's small, warm body next to mine, the sweet frailty of my baby girl cradled in my bended arm, would stop me. *Do not let your chest shake violently with crying. Hold yourself still. My friends are just afraid, afraid they'll be arrested too.*

The strain of holding in my pain exhausted me. When I closed my eyes, I saw my country burning. When I opened my eyes, I saw black emptiness. The darkness in my hut was better than the pictures in my mind.

They told him that they needed him. They lied to him.

There is a soft wind in the camp almost every night. Tonight, through the hut door I see it part the clouds.

So I will trust no one, depend on no one.

A dull, dusty hint of moonlight comes.

No one but God. No one takes God to prison. No one can starve him, shoot him, or by any other means keep him away from me.

At night there is always movement outside. People wake. Children cry. Animals root around for scraps of food. These trigger painful thoughts; I block them. But the moonlight and the breeze I welcome in. With these I feel a better Presence. Known. Familiar. Silent. But why silent? *Since the start of this brutal war You have been too silent.*

1 4

THE STILL

When you carry your own water you know the value of every drop.

WHEN MAKER WAS TAKEN, HE AND I WERE NO LONGER SHARING THE hut of Malual and Habsa. This might have made the separation from my friends appear almost normal, but everyone in camp knew that the politics of the day had changed our borders.

At the beginning of my third week of isolation, while I was boiling water and from a distance watching others work together, a slight shadow crossed my cooking fire.

"Abuk Benjamin?"

It was a teenage girl, as thin as the sticks I had gathered this morning, holding an infant on her left hip, her right hand clutching a satchel that was heavy with dust and travel.

"Abuk Benjamin?"

"Yes."

"I am the wife of your husband's younger brother."

She dropped her bag, crouched by the fire, and cradled her child. The sun lit up her face, but I could find nothing familiar in it. I had never met her or heard of her before. Her frame was slight, her features plain, her clothes worn and dirty, and her belly was swollen with another child.

"My husband was arrested too. No one wants me now either. I walked here two weeks from the camp near Assosa."

She extended her legs, exposing the torn and toughened feet that had brought her here. She lay the baby, fly-bitten and thin, across her thighs.

"Do you have water? I am so thirsty."

The silence of these weeks had dulled my tongue and cooled my heart. I filled a metal cup with water.

"Sister, do you have room for me? Can I stay with you?"

Maker's father had many wives, so Maker had many brothers and sisters that I had never met. But also in those days it was known that people came claiming to be family when they were not. Such was the desperation of the times. There was no way I could be sure, so I had never turned any away. But now that I'd been rejected myself, it would be easy to do this to another.

She was waiting for an answer.

She looked too weak to help with water or firewood. I already had too many mouths to feed. And because the hunger in my belly was also the hunger of the baby at my breast I had to feed myself too. Now a fourth and fifth mouth came begging food when soon another would be born from one of them.

"Sister, can I stay with you?" she asked again.

But I had learned that what I could not drive away, I had to welcome.

"You and your child can stay in the storage hut, over there." But the coldness of my heart toward her made me afraid.

At first the young woman was pleased to stay in the storage hut. But then at night the rats came. So in a few weeks she worked to fix up another small tent near mine. She was only a little younger than me.

"That is beautiful," she said one day, when she saw me turning a gold wrist band over and over in my palms as I calculated the needs of our compound. It was too late to try to hide it from her.

"I brought five of these with me."

"From Sudan?"

"Yes."

"Can I see them?"

I kept my hands where they were. "I have already sold three of them. I do not let go of them easily."

"Are you going to sell this one?"

It was wrought gold, engraved with a wild, fruit bearing vine that twisted its way back and forth against the two borders that were cut deep into either edge. *I will return the wrist band to a new hiding place after she puts down for the night.*

"No, I will invest it."

"How?"

"You'll see." Two weeks after her arrival I had made the decision to pull myself together and start over.

In my small compound two male orphans also stayed; they traded work for food and shelter with me. One boy was twelve, Lual, from Bar el Ghazal. The older one was Koich, who had stayed nearby the compound even while I was gone. People called young men and boys like these, who slipped into the empty spaces of every compound in the camp, the Red Army, because though hundreds of them walked out of Sudan together, orphaned when their villages were burned, soon hundreds of them would be trained to go back to fight and die.

The smaller boy helped me with firewood and simple chores. Koich did the heavy work. Many days he went for our water. We worked together to purify it. He was strong and he was generous with his strength.

One day before sunset I talked with him as we sat with the girl who called herself my sister-in-law.

"Koich, I have sold a gold band to the Ethiopians. I have enough *birr* to begin a new business, but I need you to help me get some things first."

"Tell me what things."

"We need three barrels, the big ones, from the UN."

"The ones they store the oil in?"

"Those. They throw them out sometimes. And one barrel cut down, half-size, with its lid. And three or four more big jerkanas with lids that fasten down. And we will need two more buckets."

"The buckets that the UN gives, one to a family?"

"Yes."

"How? You have yours already."

"Some people go to the UN office and say that they have lost theirs."

"I know. Then they sell them for money. Do you want me to do that?"

These buckets came sealed. They were large, with two handles and a full set of plates, cups and cooking utensils inside. If you sold a bucket-set still in its seal, you could get good money. "We are not going to sell them. We are going to use them."

"What if they see me coming twice with the same story?"

"I don't know."

My stomach turned over when I thought about doing this kind of thing.

"What else?"

"I need you to go to Gambella with me. Some others are going there soon."

"It is a day's walk. Do you really need me to go?" He cleared a space around him to sit down, already tired from this kind of thinking.

"We will buy sugar, as much as we can get with this money and are able to carry back. And yeast. At least twelve packets."

"I'll get some of the boys to go with us, then."

"And we will need a kora and two large, deep flat-bottomed pans and one funnel."

"I'm sorry, auntie, but how will we even find such things?"

It took two hard weeks of begging and buying to collect enough materials to build our alcohol still and start a new, unsanctioned business. Four weeks later we had sold enough alcohol to feed our small compound. After a few more weeks we had saved enough to reinvest.

I was brewing and selling alcohol now, the very thing I had

judged as bad in others. Now I understood their choice, because there was no choice.

"You are doing good work, my brother. I could not do this without you," I told Koich. He was showing the strain of work without a break. Each batch required a three-day cycle, with one day between batches to clean up and catch up on other things. We had already made eleven batches without stopping in forty-five days. The work was hard, but the income was good. Alcohol flowed like milk to the mouths of the desperate men of our section. Where they got the money for it, I don't know.

"This is the last packet of yeast," I told him. "After this batch we will take some days off before we go for more supplies."

The forty-sixth day was hard work, as the preparation day always was. Many extra trips to the river. Many extra trips back. Boiling water. Filtering it. Boiling water. Filtering it. Until the large holding barrel was full.

On the first day of the twelfth cycle, Koich drew out six buckets of clean water from the holding barrel and poured them one after the other into the blue barrel where the magic of fermentation took place. The rusted bands that held this barrel together were speckled brown. But we called it the blue barrel, because the paint chipping off of it was UN blue.

"Business has been good." Koich cut open a fifty-kilo sack of sugar, swung it onto his shoulder and emptied it into the water waiting in the blue barrel.

"Yes, in just a few weeks we have tripled our money," I cut the last packet of yeast open and poured it in. "But, you know, when I helped my friends with their alcohol business my first time in camp, they fired me by the end of the day!"

Koich and I took turns to stir the mixture with the long tree limb he had shaved flat for this purpose. The liquid had to be stirred well. Tired people or weak people stopped before theirs was completely mixed. Koich and I would get tired but we would never stop. Not in our body or our mind. Our product was superior because of this.

"Why did they fire you?" He dragged the stick across the bottom to bring the last of the sugar up.

"Well, they set me under a big tree with a full jerkana of alcohol." When he finished and put the stick down, I passed him the edge of a black tarp. "They said, 'You collect one birr for any vessel the size of a beer bottle.'"

"That's what you still charge, isn't it?" We spread the tarp over the open mouth of the barrel. "What did you do to get fired, drink it yourself?"

"No, Koich. You know I don't drink." We pulled the tarp down tight. He grabbed our holding rope and circled it to me. I passed my end back round to him.

"So then what?" He pulled the thick rope taut and tied it fast.

"Well, my family is well known in Wau. And my husband's family is well known in Rumbeck."

"I know." Koich tested the knot, looked up at the sun, and patted the side of the barrel for good luck.

"So, that day, everyone who saw me came up calling me cousin or sister or auntie, 'Cousin, just let me have a little. I will pay you tomorrow.' And 'Sister, you are so kind. I know your father.' I knew that meant that I must not take their money."

"So how much money did you take home at the end?" I passed him the empty yeast packet.

"It was a great day. I saw so many people I knew, and everybody came. They brought their own cups and bottles. My jerkana was empty very early."

"How much money did you make?" He asked again, folding the empty sugar sack and putting it with the other things under the tree.

"I went back to my friends with an empty jerkana and two empty hands."

"Ay, what did they say?"

"They were mad, but when I told them what happened, they had to laugh. 'It was that way with us too on our first day!' they said. But they also decided they would never send me out again, a child to the lions."

The rest of the day the mixture of water, yeast, and sugar sat sealed up under the hot black tarp, changing its nature in the blue belly of the barrel, under the burning sun. I did other chores. Koich stretched out and rested.

The second day was a heavy one. We walked the long walk to the river and back more than ten times, bringing back heavy jerkanas filled and dripping with river water. We poured them one after the other into dirty holding barrels to let the mud settle to the bottom. This water we would not drink. We would use it in another way. Exhausted, we put down early, as soon as the sun fell, because the work of the third step had to be done with precision.

So in the early morning of the third day, while the full moon was still our only light, Koich was already gathering the pans, the half-barrel, and the four clean jerkanas we were going to have filled with fresh alcohol by this time tomorrow. The jerkanas were almost as tall as my son and squared at the edges, a handle on the upper right and the spout and screw top on the left.

"Let everyone keep sleeping till the sun is high." Koich said, waving his hand high over the thousands of huts and tens of thousands of people and all the sleeping Ethiopians of the valley. "We have work to do." He stacked firewood deep, laying it in patterns to fill all the spaces between the large, round stones that formed a circle as big as the barrel's base.

Our scrubbed pans and lids and the standing river water shone bright in the soft moonlight. I was so grateful to him.

"I never asked you how you got all these things," I said.

"From the UN mostly." Koich rocked the empty half-barrel this way and that. Its hollowness scraped and banged against the stones until an agreement was made between its bottom and the circle.

"How?" I loosened the knot around the top of the fermenting barrel. Its rough body was warm to my touch. When the rope dropped, the dull, musky stench of the mixture rushed out. Its foul taste seeped into my mouth and turned my stomach over. *This bad smell will mix well with the odors of the camp and will drift to the river like a ghost before dawn. Our work will be safe.*

"I told the UN worker I needed more water barrels for my family and that my wife had lent her big pans to a friend." The two of us carefully removed the black tarp.

"Your wife?" I held the tarp at arm's length, while he pushed a bucket into the liquid darkness.

"Well, if I say I have a wife, they give me more. A person has to be clever." Koich threw me a look as he emptied one-and-a-half buckets of the warm mash into the half-barrel. He passed me the bucket but did not let go of it for a while, just smiling.

"Well, you are tall. I guess you could have a wife. And the second bucket?" I pulled the dripping tub from him. The taste it left on my hands was bitter. I would need to use soap to get it off.

"I told them that I needed it so my three kids can take baths." He took the tarp from me and passed me the metal lid.

"So, now you have three children too?" I settled the metal lid in place over the half-barrel on the stones. Koich had cut a very large round hole out of the lid's center. The fumes rose through it, burning the inside of my nostrils like fire.

"That's what I told a different worker the next day." On top of the lid Koich rested one of the broad, deep pans that he begged from the UN. He had stabbed many, many holes in its center, to match the large hole he cut in the lid on the half-barrel. "It is so hectic there, they can't even think about how to check my name off a list or even have a list."

Koich waited while I soaked rags in a paste of flour and water. We worked together slipping these between the rim of the barrel lid and the flat bottom of the pan. When the fire got hot, the paste would become cement. We had done this job together so often, we worked like one person with four arms.

"I wonder if what we are doing is stealing?" I asked, pressing the pan down as Koich positioned the *kora* inside it. The *kora* is shaped like a kind of water lily, broad and open at the top and narrow and flat at the base. It sat in the center. *Koras* were hard to get.

"Stealing! The UN should thank us for doing business and feeding ourselves." Koich places the second deep pan on top of all this to seal tight the inner chamber.

"What's in that UN tent is our raw material. We are the ones who work it and make it into something."

"But I'm just uneasy sometimes going around the rules."

"Abuk, if you follow the camp rules, two things are going to happen to you: one, you're going to get weak in your body; and two, you're going to get weak in your mind, because you're living like a begging dog. I'm not a dog. I'm a businessman."

He straightened his back and pulled matches from his pocket, his eyes flashing like stars. "My grandfather always said: 'Water that has been begged for does not quench the thirst.'"

"You begged for the barrels."

"But I work to clean the water that flows into them. And I work to make the beer that flows out of them." Koich knelt to light the fire. "Aren't I working hard enough?"

"What about me? You're not the only one working here." I saw him smile his easy smile of surrender.

"Okay, we." Koich sat back to let the fire do its magic.

At this point, the fire would heat the half-barrel, warming the mixture inside and changing the chemistry again. Once the boiling started, thick steam would rise up and creep through the holes into the inner chamber, as heat and pressure built. Then we would rush to pour cold river water into the top pan. The water on top made the steam cool down when it touched the top of the chamber. This was when transformation came, and spirits fell like rain into the open kora —the heart within the heart of the thing. This heating and sudden cooling resulted in a terrible thing that at once burned and calmed the bellies of the thirsty. This was the forbidden magic, though to us it was just work done well.

By the middle of the night, having been at this all day, Koich pushed himself to empty river water from the upper pan, bucket after bucket, pouring the heated water onto the ground. The power in his arms and the steam rising from the ground flooded the cold night with warmth. We worked for more than twenty hours and filled only three of the four jerkhanas to sell. It was the sharp edge of the night now, right next to the morning.

"You know," he said, pouring out a river bucket. "I guess you're a very great businesswoman, too."

"I have learned some things." I poured out water with him now, but I moved faster. Then we pulled and twisted the empty pan until the seal broke. Steam billowed up and we both disappeared.

"What did you learn?"

I slipped the cover back over the kora, the heart of the middle chamber, to keep its precious vapors from escaping before we poured. I knelt and opened the small spout of the last empty *jerkhana*, holding the funnel steady over it.

Carefully, with rags wrapping both his hands, Koich lifted the kora up and out, then poured the distilled spirits down the spout.

"The first week there was a man. He took the alcohol and tossed some of it into the air. If it didn't disappear before it hit the ground, then he would say, 'No, it is not strong enough. I will not buy it.'"

"Smart man." Koich knelt beside me, helping me tighten the cap. The last jerkana was full. "I'll remember that."

Koich and I leaned back against the broad tamarind tree. It was a good night—the singing crickets everywhere around us, the stars clear, filling the sky. I know the stars are fixed in their position but sometimes the earth tilts and certain ones seem closer to each other.

"One day, we had a bad time with him. He bought our alcohol and drank it right there, and then bought more and drank more, and then bought more and drank more. He stayed by me the whole day buying and drinking."

"Sounds like a good day for you both."

"Then he got up and fell forward and lay flat on his face right there in front of everyone, his arms spread out like a vulture. I thought I'd killed him."

Koich shifted and looked straight into me. I closed my eyes and my heart drifted back to Sudan, to the boyfriend I had chosen, that I wanted to marry. *How would it be to be with him now?*

"Was he dead?"

"No, but everyone thought he was. So that day I made a rule."

"What rule?"

"If you drink like that, you can never buy from me again."

"Why do you care who buys from you?"

A lone bird call pierced the night, predicting morning. The same kind of bird we had in Wau. One cried out like that when Maker's family took me. *But what can I do? I am his wife now.*

"It matters," I answered.

Koich pulled his feet up, close to mine. "So how do you keep them away?"

"I just tell them, No."

"That's all you say to them, just one word?"

"It's enough, and I've learned to say no to keep things right." I leaned forward, pulling my water basin to me to cool my face and hands.

Koich stood and picked up the blue barrel, empty now. "Anyway, I guess you can't have people dying under your tree. It's bad for business." He emptied the last of the fermented mash from the half-barrel sitting on the stones. "But what if they take it home and die there?"

I moved the last pan from the middle chamber. We peeled off the soaked rags. "I don't want anyone to die anywhere."

"That's nice, but then what are we doing here? We are making alcohol. People drink too much of it and die. Or they drink too much of it and kill." Koich set the empty top pan aside. How bad it smelled now, river water crusted on it.

"Are you blaming me, Koich?"

"I'm just saying, everyone is in pain here. Men drink to stop the pain. They drink until they fall down and then they sleep like a little child. What's wrong with that?"

"I don't drink, Koich. I work until I am too tired to worry or to wish or to feel anything. Then I collapse, too, and sleep just as deep as they do. But when the man wakes up his head pounds and his stomach is empty."

Koich watched me dry off the pans while he worked to put out the fire.

"When I wake up my head pounds, too, Koich. But I have food by me for the next day." I turned away to straighten the empty sacks and gather things to throw away.

"This is a terrible place," he said, sitting back now to rest.

"Maybe we are in hell, Koich."

"It's not hell. I know that, because the birds sing in the morning."

"So what is this place, if it's not that?"

Koich stretched out his legs, slowly, carefully, one at a time. "You know this can't be heaven, either, because we have pain. Pain proves we're not in heaven. Birds prove we're not in hell. We're in between."

"In between?"

"You know. Maybe this is the place where we get to choose."

THE NEXT RECRUITING DAY CAME SUDDENLY TO THE CAMP WITHOUT warning. Normally rumors came first, and whoever didn't want to be in the army could hide. But today hundreds of soldiers burst into our section, spreading out ten by ten. They went into every hut looking for men and boys.

"Who is in here? Come out!"

I stepped out into the sun. An SPLA soldier, with a rifle slung over his shoulder stood facing me.

"It's only me in here. Just me and my children."

He moved me aside and went in. Koich was sleeping in the kitchen hut across the way. I saw two soldiers go in there. I didn't have time to warn him. I watched them pull him out.

"I'll go but not today! I'm not ready!" he said. But they would not release him. Dut heard Koich's voice and ran to me to see what was happening.

"You're coming with us now!" they said.

I left the soldier at my hut and went over to talk with the ones holding Koich.

"Please, he is not ready." It is a terrible thing when they just take a man, with no extra clothes or food, with no tin cup to drink water from. The man or boy will go hungry before he reaches the base. He will be weak and in that condition he can be killed easily in the fighting.

"We don't have time to wait for him to think about it. He comes with us now!" They had him held in a tight grip between them. Koich motioned toward his hut.

"No, please let me help him. Just give us two minutes, and he will be ready."

"One minute." The soldiers let him go back into his hut with me.

"Tell them you'll come with them later," I said.

"It's too late for that."

We worked fast, jamming half empty bags of corn and sugar and a jar of cooking oil into an empty rice sack, along with cooking tools and a cup for water. I pushed a few UN donated clothes in on top.

"Koich, is there anything else?"

He shook his head.

"We are going to miss you." He took up his things, staring at me and Dut. That's when the soldiers' patience ran out.

"Get moving!"

My son understood something very bad was happening.

"Koich! Koich, don't go with them!" Dut cried out. Koich didn't turn around. "Koich! Come back!" Then Dut was crying hard, and I could not comfort him. Koich was to him an older brother and an uncle and a father. "Koich! Come back! Come back!"

Dut cried all that day until evening.

15

THE RIVER, THE SNAKE, AND THE YELLOW FRUIT

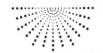

When two elephants fight, it is the grass that suffers.

SO WE LIVED THAT LIFE FOR A TIME, MY TWO SMALL CHILDREN, THE young woman I called sister-in-law, her small girl and her new baby, supporting ourselves with my now smaller business and trading and selling whatever we could find. The young woman was stronger now and able to help a bit more.

Then one day word came to me that my husband had fallen sick in prison. They told me I had to go to him, in the place where he was. They called the place Bilfam. It was an army barracks sitting on the west bank of the river that flowed between Ethiopia and Sudan. They had made part of it into a prison for traitors.

When you travel from a civilian place to a military place it is different: I had to go and ask the SPLA Chief of Staff William Nyuon for permission. He said it was no problem and signed the permission paper I carried with me to travel. He was later killed in the war.

I spent a lot of my earnings and prepared things to carry to my husband. I fried the thick biscuits you make for someone to eat and not be hungry, full of sugar and flour and oil. I packed our store of dried goat meat and maize. He sent word he didn't have a mosquito net, and so I had to buy that one too.

"Leave Dut with me," my young sister-in-law said. "But take Aker with you." Aker was just two and she was still breast-feeding.

Two SPLA soldiers found me outside my hut still putting my supplies together. "We are on our way to training in Bilfam. You will go with us."

WE STARTED THE NEXT MORNING EARLY, MY BABY AND I, ALONG with two older men and two young soldiers. One older man was Paul Anadi, and the other's name was Chagai Matte. They had battle wounds and couldn't carry much. The two young soldiers brought their guns and their bags. I brought my baby and my bags. They carried some of my small things, but the rest I carried on my head. My daughter, I tied on the front of me.

It was twelve hours walking. The air was hot. The road was dust and stones, and I was wearing closed plastic shoes. You have to wear closed shoes or the stones will slip inside your sandals and cut you. My plastic shoes on the hot road became ovens cooking my feet. They burned, and blisters came up and water came out of the blisters. But if you stopped and took your shoes off, you would never get them back on.

We reached the river by six o'clock. We were lucky on the road. All along the way my baby was so quiet; if she did cry it was a little cry, not like other children. This was good because during the day a baby's cry can wake a lion. The lion will hear you and come for you.

There was no time to rest when we got to the river. This was a crossing place. Two boatmen were helping people into their long boat. It was one-person wide and seven-persons long, so you had to get into it in a careful way. The water marks on the boatmen's long poles showed the river itself was not deep, but there were crocodile and hippo in the water. I saw the backs of some to my left downstream. I had flown in planes, helicopters, had ridden miles in military cars, vans, the swaying back of trucks. But never had I been in a boat, much less a boat in crocodile water.

When it was my time to get in, the boat lurched and began to shake wildly. It went off balance, this way and then that, wanting to throw us in.

The boatman yelled at me, "Get out, woman, you're going to get us all killed!"

It wasn't me, it was my body shaking with great violence and rocking the boat so wildly. All my fears had come together in that instant, like nails suddenly drawn to a magnet. All the fears that I'd been holding off until now: fear from bullets flying past, fear from newborn babies and their mothers dying, fear from long nights holding my breath while my young boy gasped for air.

"Woman!" They took my baby and grabbed my two hands hard. "Get out of this boat now!" The two soldiers pulled me back to the shore.

The soldiers told the boatmen, "Take her baby across!"

The soldiers held me down while they took my baby. "What's wrong with you?" they said.

No one was happy at all with me. But, now seeing my baby on the other side, no one was more unhappy than I. Now I would have to steady myself if I wanted to see her again.

Not one person would go into the boat with me after that. So the boatmen came back and put me alone in the middle and told me, "Put your legs crossed like this. Close your eyes and think that you are sitting at a table having tea with your husband." I held the two sides of the boat hard and squeezed my eyes shut and kept praying a frightened prayer while the water hissed past, until I felt the boat hit shore on the other side.

The place where we came aground was not flat like where we'd set off. It was a dirt cliff, straight up, and tall like the height of a man. I had to pull my way up, grabbing onto roots and shoving my feet into the holes that other travelers had made. *They need to fix this!* When my shoulders showed up over the top, men pulled me the rest of the way. A woman gave my baby back to me, into my arms. Then all the people around us threw their heads back and cheered.

This plateau was a guarding place. All of us who crossed could rest here for a while. Under a tree there was a small fire boiling water to make tea. Some soldiers lived here like a family and watched over the river for enemies.

"Uncle, can I bring you some tea?" I asked an old man who had joined us on the road, once we were settled. I was worried for him. He was not doing well. I had my tea leaves and sugar and maize with me. But there were only two metal cups in the whole camp. I poured tea for two people, then we all waited for it to cool and for them to drink. And then I poured more into the same cups for another two people, and we all waited again, until all had shared in the tea. I broke some hard cookies for them to share as well. And after that I had my tea, too. This was our Sudanese way.

By late that night we finally reached the base at Bilfam. They had brought my husband down to the smaller lodgings there because of his lung sickness. Before we could enter, though, they checked us from head to foot and went through all our things. More waiting, more weariness, more worry. Then a woman I had known back in Itang came. Her husband was working at the base. She came and took me to her house. There, my baby and I slept gratefully till morning.

The next day they took me to the place where my sick husband lay. There was little in his eyes to greet me or his child. But we talked. He had always been asthmatic, but now he had more than asthma. He told me that in the big prison they beat him and the other men often, and tied them up in bad ways. On some days they held his head under water and brought it out and put it back in time after time. That's when he got too sick to stay there.

My old friend and I started cooking every morning, pooling our maize and dried meat and flour together, bringing food to my husband. That made him popular. Soon a dozen or more men joined in to share his breakfast, military men who knew him, not prisoners. His spirit began to rally as our cooking chores increased. I saw my husband happy again with his old friends. On these mornings they didn't care about which side they were on in the war. They loved the food and they loved each other. That was all.

But I had to go back to my camp soon. The rainy season was starting up, and the river was swelling. I was thinking too much about my son.

So my husband asked them to make arrangements.

"There is a car that comes from the east down to the river every two days with supplies. They bring maize and send it on the boat to our camp. Go early. I will send an escort with you. They will take you in the car back to Itang." That was all.

That was all. A man introduced himself to me in the morning and said, "We need to go." My baby and I went with him to the river crossing. This time neither the boat nor my body shook, and we crossed well. Then we settled in to wait on the other side, believing the car would come.

We waited there until nighttime. But instead of a car coming for us, mosquitoes came. On a night like that you can't shoo them away, because the air rings thick with them like rain. You have to wipe them off your arms like water. I had a small cloth to cover my daughter's face and legs, but she was still crying, "Mama, Mama."

We waited all night, hungry, troubled, and eaten by mosquitoes. When the promised car came the next day, others got into it right away. Then more who were waiting with us talked to the driver, and he let them hang on to the side to go back with him. But he refused me.

"It's too risky for you and the baby."

My escort took the driver aside to beg more.

The driver asked him, "Whose wife is she?"

"Maker Benjamin's wife."

"Then I definitely will not take her!"

When I heard this, I begged loudly from a distance, "Please, please, let me hang on to the side. I can do it!"

The driver refused.

As the car drove away, heavy with people and swaying this way and that, I called again, "I can do it. Give me a chance." Then they were gone.

It was late afternoon when a small breeze started up, cooling and calm. The mosquitoes withdrew, and all the place became still and quiet, as did my heart, my little girl, and my guard. But slowly the breeze waxed stronger and got colder and then gave way to a hard wind like a great wall pressing down on us. Then, lightning cut through the sky, and heavy rain broke down upon us, pouring and pounding—a river from the sky with no shore. The hard wind forced rain into our eyes, our mouths, and our bones. We held onto exposed roots in the ground to not be swept away. I strapped my daughter tight around me.

Hours later the endless storm came to an end, as troubles always do. The ground was soaked by that time. Night was here, and we heard animal sounds and growling in the forest. But we had to sleep. My escort had been given no gun to take with him and he was mad. We pounded sticks into the ground and strung a net. Under it, we spread plastic to sleep on and we laid down. But my body was awake. My skin was remembering the biting mosquitoes and the pounding rain, and my mind turned to memories instead of sleep.

So I barely realized what was happening until the creature was already moving up my body and was at my ribs, undulating upward.

"Something big is on me," I whispered to the guard.

"Stay still." He breathed the word "snake" and fell silent.

It moved upward toward my extended arm, flattening my ear as it passed. It weighed heavily on my chest as it moved along. Then I felt the tail of it graze my face. And it was gone.

"Which way did it go?" he asked me.

"Toward the river, I think." Now I could tremble and shake and pull my baby close under me.

"It was probably one of those big snakes the river people make shoes from," he said. "Go back to sleep."

I also knew about those snakes. People say they bite and wrap themselves around a person to kill them. So I decided I was going to stay awake now, I was going to stay alert now, and I did so as long as I could.

The next morning my guard shook me to wake me. I jumped up. "Another animal!" I thought. His human form was barely visible in the small light of dawn.

"Let's go now. It's still cool. We have to leave this place," he said.

I put the plastic shoes back on my feet. I could do this now because my feet had healed up at the base. But it had been about two days now since I'd eaten, the same since I'd slept well.

"There's no time to cook. We must go." He raised my bags to his shoulder. We had to move on, this time walking.

By the time the sun was straight up above and the top of my head and the bottoms of my feet were burning hot, we passed near a soldier camp. The voices of men in the language of Dinka and the smells of their cooking were in the air. We called to them and asked if we could rest there a while. They received us and cleared a place in a back hut for me and my daughter to lie down. They were kind to us, protective, but my stomach groaned for the maize and dried meat they were cooking.

In our tradition, it is not right to ask for food or even say that you are hungry when the people near you are cooking. It is shameful to do this. But a person can hope they will offer. I fell asleep hoping, while my guard sat with the men.

As I slept, my blood was still pumping with anger and sadness at this life. I dreamed a kind of vision. I was standing above a crowd of people shouting at them to choose peace over war, love over hate. But my voice was being drowned out by a man who was yelling at me to step down.

"Madame, it's time!" My escort was yelling in the doorway of the hut. "Get down from your bed! We need to get going now. It is late."

My knees and my back were weak, but my feeling of duty was strong enough to make me stand. I rose, tied my daughter to my body, picked up my things, and turned my feet to the road. "Yes, let's get going," I said. I had nursed my daughter, but I hadn't eaten myself. I could feel a shaking coming up into my arms.

ABOUT FOUR HOURS LATER, AHEAD OF US DOWN THE ROAD, I SAW THE dark, leafy branches of a great, spreading tree. I saw women with their babies sitting under it amid baskets woven the way Nuer people weave. Their voices bubbled like a waterfall. Shade spread out like a beautiful cloth underneath them.

With their permission I sat down. I had learned to speak Nuer in

Itang, from all the bartering we women did together. So now I told them "Thank you" in their language.

"This lady, she is too hungry," one woman said. "Look at her trembling."

"And she has a small baby," another said.

"This lady, she can die." One woman took a bright yellow dried fruit from her basket. "And they've been walking."

"Here, lady, take this fruit." She put it in my hand. "Chew it like candy. There's a hard seed in it. Crush it and suck the juice. Spit out nothing."

An older one asked for my baby and cradled her. "This baby is okay. She has been eating from your breast."

They could tell that the man with me had eaten and told him, "This is women's fruit," so that he would be ashamed to want it.

"Lady, this is your time to eat," said another. "Crush the seed between your teeth now." I used the teeth in the back of my jaw to do this.

The dark curtain that had fallen in front of my eyes pulled back and light came into my thoughts. I felt energy rise slowly through my limbs, steadying me and giving me back my life.

I had forgotten what it felt like to be alive and to have the kind of strength that knows its own direction. The fruit also took away the pain that had slowed my walking down. I chewed more of it and gave it, softened by my own teeth, to my baby. Her eyes brightened too.

"There, the lady's coming around!" They clapped their hands and called out. "Now let the baby have another bite."

They called the fruit *lalop* I think, but I don't remember well. And they gave me two more pieces of whole fruit to take with me on the road. I have looked for that kind of yellow fruit everywhere since but have never found it, and I have never found women like these again either, not anywhere, welcoming and kind, like they had known me my whole life. I said thank you to them again and again, in Dinka and in Nuer, many times over, before we left.

Now I was alive on my feet, and my baby was content. We walked into Itang in peace before nightfall. When I remember back now, I love those women so much—those sweet women of the Nuer, appearing under a great, spreading tree, loving me as one of their own. Do angels appear in the form of Nuer?

As I approached my small compound at Itang, Dut ran to me from the side of the young woman who called herself my sister-in-law. These were the ones who welcomed me now. An orphaned boy or two looked up from the cooking fire, ashamed to be seen preparing food. Cooking is a woman's role and a man must not do it if he is to be called a man. But they were boys, and in the camp so many things were already broken down and reversed. What was one more broken thing?

But from so many experiences I had become quite sensitive to danger. Though I saw they were okay, I felt a tension in the air. More than tension. It was fear.

"Auntie Abuk!" the older boy, Agok, called to me. "It is good you were not here!"

"What is it?"

"A boy was killed," he said.

"Shot with a rifle," the other added. "Some boys were fighting over a ball. That ball you made for your son out of rags."

"There are many rifles in the camp now. We found some," Agok looked down. "But we can't let the men know we've found them."

"But the one boy, he got so angry. He went to a hiding place and pulled one out."

"And he shot the boy who kept the ball from him, down by the water barrel. He fell right there." Agok pointed to a compound not far from ours.

"It was terrible. The bullet hit the barrel too, and water spilled and made his blood spread farther. It soaked into the ground and stained it. We had to kick dust over it while the other boy ran and hid his rifle."

"There was a lot of trouble. A lot of yelling from the men."

"You were in the fight, too?"

"No, auntie." They both looked away. "No one cried for him, auntie."

In the camp, time had a way of moving in its own direction, sometimes forward, sometimes backward. Sometimes it slithered sideways like a snake, and you felt like you had been in that time before.

The air had shifted. More men of army age were coming and going, no longer hiding so carefully in the bush. More stories of rifles buzzed everywhere like flies over flesh. And there were rumors that SPLA soldiers had conducted raids against the local villagers, stealing animals and crops.

Another rumor came, too. People told me my father had been in prison since the year Aker was born. Why was I just now hearing of this? He was accused of being a "political intellectual." He did not want the war, so he was put in a place where his voice would not be heard. Rumors of conspiracies multiplied in the camp. The SPLA command had completely split now, and each side arrested more and more men from the other.

It was also said that Garang was on his own now and had sided with Mengistu, president of Ethiopia. Garang led raids for him against Ethiopian rebel forces near the camps. How long would it be before retaliation comes to us? We who had fed those South Sudanese soldiers—those soldiers who were our husbands and brothers?

Maker had been wrong when he said that no one cared about this place, that war would never come here. Where soldiers go, war always follows.

We all felt the danger growing, within the camp and without. I had always used the nighttime to try to rest my body, to have my children near me so they would know a mother's touch. But night and day also had shifted in the camp, and people began to take turns to hold vigil day and night.

This was not a guarding vigil with rifles or with fire. It was a holy vigil they kept with song and dance and prayers. They did this to turn up the light in the camp, so the angels might see us from far away and so God might rise up and come.

It is nighttime now in the camp, but the singers are awake. They will pray until dawn, then at dawn they will sleep and others will fill their place, each taking their turn to stand and cry out.

I have not joined them before, but this night fears are swarming my heart, biting and sucking the sleep from my veins. It is useless to hope for rest. So I rise to join the singers in their meeting by the river.

A man throws his head back and sings high, "God, you are God at all times."

The people clap their hands and answer, "*God, you are God at all times.*"

The drummers drum, stick on stick. The people clap hand on hand; their feet move left, move right.

Another man sings: "In Elijah's time you answered by fire."

All the people sing: "*God, you are God at all times.*"

Their hands clap twice the beat of my heavy heart. The song's pulse quickens mine.

One voice: "In Moses' time you opened the sea."

All: "*God, you are God at all times.*"

The breaths of scores of people merge in the night air.

The man calls again, "In the time of sickness you heal me."

"*God, you are God at all times.*"

Like wind through the trees, their song passes through me—bends me low like a willow, lifts me high like the leaves.

"In the time of sadness, you come to me."

"*God, you are God at all times.*"

Their words give voice to places in me where I've never found words before. Tonight, my voice and my hands touch the night sky with theirs. I must bring this hope home to my children. As I walk back to my hut, peace walks home with me and it stays with us till morning comes.

IT WAS 1991. BEFORE THE ITANG MASSACRE LATER THAT YEAR, MY husband convinced someone to take me and my children to a refugee place in the capital of Kenya. Later, I was told by survivors about the attack that followed. Early one morning Ethiopian fighters charged the camp from the east, hordes of them, armed and angry. They drove everyone, running, screaming toward the river that separates South

Sudan from their country. Many of my friends and orphaned boys I had fed died that day in the massacre. They died running from camp, they drowned in the river, they died being shot while trying to swim across. Even some were shot after they reached the other side. There was no mercy.

I heard that Anip, my high school friend who had given birth with me in Addis, had left her baby behind to join the SPLA and take revenge for her husband's death. They said she fought valiantly that day at the river. The SPLA soldiers with her told her to go to a shallow place where they were crossing others but she would not turn her back on the enemy to run. Instead, she fired all the bullets in her gun until she herself was shot dead and fell into the river too. Her body was carried downstream with so many others. They say her body was never found.

There are two kinds of peace that I know of, one in life and one in death. That day, I believe Anip found hers.

16

TWO CITIES AND THE BIRTH OF A NATION

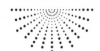

*Happiness requires something to do, something to love, and
something to hope for.*

IT WAS OVER A THOUSAND MILES FROM ITANG TO NAIROBI. TWO LONG
days over good roads and bad roads, stopping to lay our tired bodies
down along the way. But it was good to go to Nairobi. Nairobi had
everything Itang did not. And a good woman there, Amal Athahar, a
friend's wife, received me and made room for me and my small children in her place and helped to hide us. It had been my day and night
dream to put my son in school, but a refugee child was not welcome
there. So she registered my son in her name.

In those days in Nairobi, all new arrivals had to look out for the
police. If they saw you were a Sudanese, they would arrest you and
put you in prison. We had no permission to be in their country. But
here we were, hungry and homeless. In the long run, there was still a
way. If they put you in prison, you had only to find someone to pay
money, and they would let you go. I was lucky, too. People said I
looked like a Kenyan woman; they said I could go out on the street
without trouble. But, even so, I did not go out except for the most
needed things. It was best to not be seen.

My sister-in-law in Canada, Margaret Benjamin, sent us $200 a month. That was a lot of money—enough to keep my son in school and for me to give something to my friend.

In 1992, Maker got out of prison in Sudan and came to Nairobi with others who had found a way out. He had no place to stay, so he stayed with us. But he had been hurt badly by many things, stripped of his power, his voice in the world silenced. Only alcohol could take away his pain now, but it passed it on to us, his wife and children.

The ACROSS program, an international Christian organization working in Nairobi, had helped us settle into a small place of our own. There, my youngest daughter Sahra was born, in August 1993, a tiny, unexpected blessing—and another mouth to feed. After that, the small rooms could not easily hold us all.

One day, when Maker's anger and unrest had become too much, when we could house him and calm him no more, a friend came to me with timely news. "Abuk, your name has been posted! Your name is on the list of people called to interview with the UNHCR!"

"My name? How do they know me?" I had lost track of so many things in the daily stir of survival. I did not remember that I had put my name in for resettlement over three years before. I had put my name on so many lists I could not remember them all.

"It is true. You must go!"

Maker's name had not been posted, only mine, which also included by default my three children. It would be no great hardship on him now, though, to be left behind. He was already finding a way to get his voice back on the radio through the BBC. From this point on, other than a brief, unsuccessful attempt to rejoin together as a family a few years later, Maker went his own way and his story was no longer mine to tell. He passed away in 2021.

ON AUGUST 31, 1994, MY SMALL CHILDREN AND I BOARDED A flight with other refugees destined for the United States. But we did not know exactly where we would land or how we would live. Our flight stopped in New York at midnight. With no explanation, they loaded us and everything we owned onto an old bus that was ready to give out too, weary from its own travels. We watched through the windows as we passed darkened streets, buildings with broken windows, their walls painted with crude words, men lined up against them alongside their empty bottles. Where were they taking us? This place was poorer than Nairobi.

To cut through the mood one traveler shouted, "Welcome to America!"

We all laughed because that's what you do when things look so bad that you have to let it out. Finally the bus pulled up to a well-lit hotel. They handed us our things and told us to spend the night there because the next day we would all be going to different cities. We laughed a different laugh then, grabbing our things.

My next flight landed in Dallas. When we deplaned that afternoon, a small Asian man picked me and my children out from the crowd. I don't know how this man recognized us. It may be that we just looked lost, or because I was holding four World Bank bags containing everything that gave us a right to be here—our documents, our passports, and our applications for asylum. In those days my English was still not strong, and maybe his was not either, but when I looked at him, I knew the meaning of his smile and his extended hand, and the tilt of his head toward the direction we would go. His sign had the letters IRC, which I later learned meant International Rescue Committee.

He drove us in his own small car to a complex of tall buildings standing together like a village, with flat roofs and three or four floors of balconies with bicycles, potted plants, old chairs, and stairs going up and down on the outside. He walked us up to a small apartment on the second floor.

"Here you are," he said. There was carpet on the floor and a folding table in the center holding a laundry basket full of soaps, pots, pans, plates, canned and boxed foods, towels. Simple furniture lined the walls. It smelled of bleach, like the hospital in Addis.

"Here is your key. Someone will come for you in a few days." And he was gone.

Before we left Nairobi, Sahra, just one year old, had refused to learn to walk. Maybe the floors had been too rough for her or maybe there was nowhere she wanted to go. We would stand her up, and she would sit back down. No one could convince her to try. But now we were in the US. That first day, we felt so tired from our travels and so glad to be in something we could call our own, we went down with the sun. The next morning, before we knew anything or even had our eyes opened very wide, Sahra was already up and walking along the furniture, curling her toes in the carpet, talking softly to herself. She had waited to take her first steps here, in Dallas.

AROUND THAT TIME, SOUTH SUDAN WAS ALSO TAKING ITS FIRST unsteady steps toward freedom. In 1994, the SPLM held its first convention to define the terms of a new relationship with the North. In fits and starts over the next few years, ceasefires were made and broken, peace talks restarted and stopped again until, finally in 2005, a Comprehensive Peace Agreement (CPA) with the Khartoum government was reached. In 2008, in part to address failed plans and in part to prepare for the scheduled elections of 2009, a second SPLM convention was announced. By this time, I had become active in leadership in the SPLM Women's League in the US. I was invited to be a delegate and help organize the convention. I would be flown back to Juba, the capital city of South Sudan. It was my chance to go back home and, even more, I believed it would be my chance to take part in shaping a new country.

I did indeed renew old ties and build new relationships face-to-face with other women of the diaspora and of the new South Sudan. There was much hope among us. But our voices were not to be heard at that time or to have influence in the decisions of men. We had been invited just to serve and to celebrate with them. It would be years before the bonds we women were forming would hold power enough to move the country.

When the convention ended, though, I was free to stay on. My children were old enough now to be on their own in the States for a while.

Through all my years in exile, the memory of one person was always with me, a voice in my heart guiding me. Twenty-five years ago, I had been separated from my mother because of war. Now after so long a time I could return to my birthplace to see her big smile again.

The day I arrived in Rumbek in 2008, she gave directions to my driver by cell phone to find the dirt road by her place. When we got there, she had the phone in one hand and was holding onto a small cow with the other. She opened her arms to greet me, and the cow got away. So the villagers who had come to see me ran off to get it back. We started our visit laughing and did not say much to each other at first about the bad days. This was our way to keep our new joys clean from the stain of old troubles.

But, eventually, we had to speak of those things.

"Abuk when you sent money from the US for us to leave for Uganda, you have no idea what you saved us from."

I had worked jobs in Dallas with overtime to send money back home. But I wasn't used to the way things were done. After a month in our apartment, the IRC told me, "We're not paying the rent anymore. You have to work now. Leave your baby with the neighbors down the way." My neighbors were an exiled couple from Liberia; the woman was old and her husband was blind. "We've already talked to them. They're happy to take Sahra." It was true. They were good people and they did their best with her, with kindness and with love.

My first job was at a cleaners, a place loud with machines, with stifling heat, with no place to sit and talk to the people around you while you worked. There was an older woman there I kept my eye on. I said, "As long as she's standing I will stay on my feet too." But I couldn't do it. After a few ten-hour days and being too long away from Sahra, I stopped going. The IRC got angry with me. So I went to work at the county hospital. It was a better job, cleaning rooms. I got to know people there from different countries, some higher rank, some lower, some doctors, some cleaners, and we made friends. Then I worked assembling semiconductors; I made friends there too, with people from everywhere. So many colors, so many languages. This was the kind of world I wanted my children to grow up in. I worked hard in that job, for my children and for my mother back in Sudan.

"You didn't tell me what was really happening, Mother. When I sent you money, I thought you were going to Uganda for your health."

"For my health! Ha!" she leaned back. "For our lives!"

"I didn't know how bad it was getting for you."

"This small town was like a goat where one man pulls it hard by the horns and another man pulls it harder by the tail. The rebel army came for our crops, then the government army came for the rebels, beating us to find out where they were hiding."

I felt bad for her. Life had been bad for me, but there was no war where I was. I did not know then that in a few short years I, like her, would be caught in the crossfire.

"Why didn't you go to Australia with my brother when you had a chance to go?"

"I couldn't, Abuk. Your brother here was killed, and his children were left behind. I had to go back to my grandchildren and other little ones like them. Without me, they were just eggs in an empty nest without a hen to hatch them."

I had brought many things with me for her and for my family there. But when our visit was over and I had to go back to my own children, I gave her my best gift: two large bottles of aspirin to keep for herself. Afterwards I heard that she became known as the village doctor because whenever people became sick, she would take out one bottle and give each person an aspirin. People walked from far away just to see her for that. My mother loved to make a difference. And she loved to make people laugh.

In 2011, I watched events unfolding in South Sudan from the cool of our small apartment in Dallas. In my home country, shade was a wonderful thing, valued above so many things—the shade of a great tree, the shade of a standing wall or market tent—shade against the burning sun, the noonday heat. But here, in our second-floor apartment, my curtains, thick and floral, stood in for the shade of a tree and formed a cocoon that wrapped me and my children well. But they gave little cover from the news streaming in on our TV.

According to the 2005 accord between the Khartoum government and the SPLA in the south, a referendum was to take place in 2011 to determine the people's will for independence. But before the vote could be taken, I and over a million of our countrymen now scattered throughout the world, and millions of our internally displaced peoples and countless nomadic tribesmen, and the rest of our surviving peoples in the south had to be taken into account somehow.

In Darfur, the Justice and Equality Movement and other groups threatened to attack census takers. Displaced South Sudanese hid from the count out of fear of becoming visible to the government. How could a census be taken and votes counted under such conditions?

A minimum of 60 percent of eligible voters had to turn out for the referendum vote to be honored. To achieve this in the most direct way, in-country voter registration began in mid-November 2010. Thanks to the tireless work of multi-agency mobilization, five million made it to register before the deadline. By January 2011, far-flung polling places had also been set up for South Sudanese refugees in Darfur, as well as in eight other countries that held large refugee populations, including the United States and Canada.

In February 2011, though in some places the number of ballots was more than the number of voters, the vote was declared in favor of independence from Khartoum. I traveled to Washington, DC, for the great day of celebration—July 9, 2011—when South Sudan officially became the world's newest nation. It was a day filled with dancing, speeches, tears, and the joyful sounds of people at peace after so many years. The war was finally over, and rebuilding could begin.

17

SHADOWS IN THE WATER

Do not think there are no crocodiles just because the water is calm.

I WENT BACK TO SOUTH SUDAN AGAIN IN 2012 FOR MY DAUGHTER
Aker's wedding, my heart full of hope for her and for my country. It
was a celebration time. She had graduated from university in the US
and had gone back to Juba to work in the Deng Foundation, an organization dedicated to making access for all the disabled—those
disabled from birth or by war—to register to vote in the independence
referendum. She had met her husband there. After their beautiful
wedding on August 4, 2012, I stayed on in Juba for another year to
enjoy this new time of peace, planning to then go back to Dallas for
Christmas with Dut and Sahra.

It was December 15, 2013, days before my flight would leave.
Aker and her husband were staying with her husband's family in Hai
Amarat, not far from the airport. I was with my sister Adhieu and our
uncle Nun that night, sitting out on the veranda in the cool of the
evening. My sister and I had rented this home together. It had two
bedrooms and a dividing wall. She had invited her uncle Nun from
his village, Twic, maybe four hundred miles from Juba. He was the
youngest of many brothers, a good man and funny, and when he
drank he got so happy and so loud.

Our veranda floor was tiled in shades of white and brown, patterned like an opening flower. It shone like polished marble in the evening lights. In our garden out back, we sat in plainer chairs and raised eggplant, tomatoes, and corn, which we shared with our neighbors and with green caterpillars, uninvited guests. I watered this garden every day. It was my joy.

THAT NIGHT, WE WERE RELAXING IN OUR SOFT, FLORAL FURNITURE out front on the veranda, listening to music on the radio. Around 9 p.m., we suddenly heard gunshots. First from this side, then from that. In the soft glow of the streetlights, we saw bullets streak across the sky—maybe eight hundred or a thousand feet from us and coming closer. The people who had been strolling in the streets started running in directions that made no sense.

At first, my relaxed mind could not put these things together. But soon I was running, too—like them, running to any place I could reach right away for safety.

I ran inside our rented house, bending down so the bullets meant for tall fighting men would not strike me. My sister and uncle ran into the other side of the house and closed the door behind them.

In their rush they had left the radio outside on the patio. I had left my phone.

Now hiding in my side of the house, I had no way to reach others; no way to know why the fighting had started. Only my two ears and my own skin could inform me now.

The wall inside the house kept me apart from my uncle and sister. But we could call to each other through it. My uncle told me to get down under the bed but I was already there, holding my pillow tight against me because when you don't have a gun or a vest you grab what you can, even if it's a foolish thing.

When we ran inside at the first shots, our relative Gabriel called my uncle and told him, "Do not leave the house." Gabriel was military, a man often on the front line, and knew the orders. More people started calling after that, so my uncle's phone kept on ringing loudly.

My sister told him to turn his phone off, "People will hear us!" But it was a new phone and he didn't know how to silence it. So my sister tore it apart and threw the battery aside.

I heard a door slam outside, screaming, the cries of children, and the footfalls of a family running. Then a machine gun and a bigger scream, "Aawwww!"

I heard the voices of men outside, shouting in the Nuer tongue: "Go to the other side. There are more of them, they're running!" Because the Nuer men outside might hear our Dinka words and then break in to kill us too, we shut our mouths. Even uncle Nun, even with the evening's drink inside him, held his peace.

An explosion shook our street. Bullets from machine guns were falling on our metal roof like bad rain. I heard the grinding of a heavy tank. But my heart beat faster and heavier than all of these. *God, give us another chance. I don't want to lose more people. Let this fighting stop!*

For a long time, I heard a man by our outside wall groaning; then after a time his groaning stopped. Sometimes I heard Nuer soldiers cry out, too. I have learned the sound when a bullet goes into a body. Not the usual *pow-pow*; when it hits the body, the sound is dull and stops short.

The shooting came to a lull after midnight for maybe thirty minutes and then resumed. I stayed trembling under the bed clutching that pillow all night as the shooting dragged on. Even when the sound of gunfire stopped for a time, we stayed down.

It was a time for thinking. Just days before this, I had been standing shoulder to shoulder with hopeful women dreaming to breathe new life into our country. Now I was hiding from gunfire alone, trembling on the ground alone, worrying to save my own life alone, with fear for my newlywed daughter's life pounding in my ears louder than gunfire.

In the morning we heard soldiers shouting outside in a different voice, in Dinka. So we knew we could speak across the wall again but the come-and-go shooting kept up into early afternoon, so we did not dare to move from our places or go to a window to look. Our uncle did not drink at all that day and kept his peace.

At about 2:30 p.m., we finally heard civilian people on the street talking back and forth and we went outside. What I saw when I stepped out, I do not want to put into your mind. It is not something to be spoken of, or to be made into memories. But of the people still moving about on their feet, I saw women and children step carefully, sometimes slipping, carrying their things, bringing goats and chickens along with them, to flee that place while saving whatever they had left.

My neighbor-friend at the time had five beautiful children. I called her to tell her she should get into a car with us now, but there was no answer. The time of the screaming of children last night, I hoped it had not been them.

We had to get out now. With yesterday's clothes still on me, I grabbed my purse and my phone from the veranda. Only that. On the way, our uncle saw drinks set out for a wedding, but there would be no wedding today. He was gathering up some bottles to take with us. "No, leave them and come!" we told him, "There is no time to stop for anything, anyone." *Dear God, please help my friend and her children!*

WE MADE IT TO OUR CAR BUT WHERE WOULD WE GO? HAD THIS BEEN just a tribal fight or had the new government been overthrown? Where would we go? I had been working with a young lady at the Chamber of Commerce. Many of us had been working there, women working together, volunteering, organizing, being trained by the World Bank to cultivate young businesses. I called her, and she said to come. But her house was already full of frightened people.

We drove toward the hotel Nile Comfort Inn where we had a cousin working. Every turn was blocked by soldiers, but the soldiers had Dinka markings on their faces and let us through. It took hours to go forward just one inch. For a moment, we thought to go back but people near us said, "No! You will be killed if you go back there."

We feared there would be no room in the hotel for us either but, "We will put it in God's hands," I said.

When we got there, our cousin made a place for us. That's when my daughter Aker's call got through. She had been crying all night trying to reach me. She lived in a safer part of the city but she had felt no peace. Through her tears she told me to go to the US embassy. She had registered with the Embassy before leaving the US and now they were texting her saying a flight would leave on the eighteenth to take American citizens out of danger. Aker could go, but her husband would have to stay. I could go, but my sister and uncle would have to stay.

On December 16th, shooting started again, this time by the airport. We hoped it would not reach us where we were. It's the cross-fire that you fear; they are not shooting at you, but the bullets that aren't meant for you will still kill you.

We still had no working radio, so through the night we got our news by phone. Terrible news. Word came to us that people we knew, so many of them, had been killed. But we also heard that a strong woman, the chef at a big restaurant, was making food at her home for people pinned down by the fighting.

Even so, we decided not to go out to the street, not even to eat.

But on the last day, the eighteenth, we went out, straight through the streets, not stopping until we reached the airport. It was now a safe zone, surrounded by government troops. A charter plane was waiting, engines churning. There we found Aker and her husband, my friend Akuot and her children. Our hair ungroomed, our clothes days old, our shoes stained. When we met, our tears poured down like rivers, washing our faces and blotting out the sight of everything before and beyond that sweet moment together. We held on to each other until we couldn't anymore because the ones staying behind had to send us on.

Fear had wound itself around me like a snake and would not let me let go. I sat pressed against Aker on the plane, promising to never be apart again. I was thinking too much: *We will be hijacked. They will shoot us down.* (Something that did happen to another plane later on.) But our plane eventually got high enough. There would be no more harm to us today but, even so, nothing could make me feel that we were safe. After four days of fear, every drop of courage had been sweated out of me.

Soon I was back in the US, but still hearing the news from my country. I found out that the fighting we had heard that night was the start of a new brother-on-brother war, our right hand against our left, between our Nuer brother Riek Machar and our Dinka brother Salva Kiir. They had been tasked to form a new government together. But their top skill, perfected over so many years, was only to fight and make war.

I lost many people as this feud continued: cousins, uncles, people on both sides of my family, both Dinka and Nuer. Every time the phone rang in my Dallas apartment, I breathed deep before I answered. But in 2015, a different kind of call came, saying that my mother had been injured in Rumbek. She had been in the forest gathering firewood, and a branch she pulled on fell hard on the top of her head. We gathered money from all our relatives and sent her to a hospital in Khartoum, where machines could see inside her and tell us what was wrong. They found a blood clot in her brain. They said that in her seventies she was too old to survive a surgery, so they put her on medicine for the next year and a half, while she stayed with my older brother in the north.

Then I got the call that she had collapsed again and lay for days in a coma in the Khartoum hospital. When she awoke, she just told them, "Take me back to Rumbek. I want to go there as myself. I won't go there in a box." My brother in Australia sent money, and she returned to her home place. Her mind was still good, but sometimes when we were talking on the phone, thousands of miles apart, she suddenly would say to me, "Who is this?"

Then I got the call that she had passed away. Her grandchildren and some women of the family were having coffee around her bed, laughing and joking with her. She was the great jokester of our family. Then she suddenly sat up and asked them, "Where is Abuk? Is she really in America?" and gave them a handful of money to go find me, which made them laugh too. Not long after, though, she died holding the youngest child. The child told me later, "Auntie, Aboba fell asleep while she was holding my hand."

18

WOMEN MAKING PEACE

When the sleeping women awake, mountains move.

THOUGH FIGHTING HAD BEEN FIERCE BETWEEN DINKA AND NUER since that December day in 2013, a peace deal was signed in 2015, and in the spring of 2016, Riek Machar, leader of the opposing forces that had been expelled from Juba, accepted the invitation to return to the capital with his army to join the new government. The number of guns in Juba increased greatly with their arrival, so the government set up checkpoints to inspect every vehicle and question anyone they found armed. The official word was that this was done to reduce violent crime in the city.

I went back to Juba in 2017 for a brief stay during this new time of peace. One day we were driving through the city on our way back from a meeting for the growth of women-owned businesses, as life on the street had become almost normal again. Except for the checkpoints.

"Just let me deal with this." Justin, our driver said, putting his hand to his lips to silence us. We'd arrived at another checkpoint. A big bus had been stopped and was being boarded by armed soldiers.

"Get down from there, all of you!" the guards shouted. There were more soldiers at this checkpoint than at the others. I felt something different in their voices—something raw, tense.

Passengers emerged, voices low, feet dragging. Who knows how many checkpoints they had already been through?

"Hurry up!" the soldiers said.

Our driver got concerned. "We can't stay here." He slid his hand to the gear shift and put his foot down on the gas. My sister was in a car behind us at the checkpoint. Her driver chose to wait.

It was unusually cold out, like the world gets sometimes before a storm breaks. I saw soldiers standing at the roadside shivering and felt bad for them.

"I'm getting us out of here." Justin eased our small car down a side road and then swiftly inside the gate of the place where we were staying.

"Keep the car in here." We thanked him and wished him safety as he left. I was glad to be inside our walls. I just needed some tea and some time to settle.

But before the water could reach a boil, we heard machine guns break out in the direction of the checkpoint. Then a series of explosions shook the ground, rattling the teacups I had just set down.

The phone rang. It was my daughter, "Mom, we hear fighting outside!" She was closer to the airport. Then my sister, whose car had also been stopped, burst through the door out of breath. "They started shooting right in front of us! People being killed right in their cars. We got out and ran!"

"Are you hurt, sister?"

"No, I'm okay."

Over the next hours the bombs hit closer and the gunfire grew more intense, to the point you could not hear the individual shots anymore. Our house shook with every bomb. Our country's fragile peace was shattering all around us. Who would gather up the pieces this time? Would any pieces be left to gather?

But then around 9 p.m., the sky above us answered back in anger. Sudden thunder crashed louder than the bombs. A now-raging storm lit up the sky like day, again and again. And then the final strike came —a great, blinding bolt of lightning, and in the same instant a bone-shattering boom. The bones of our house and the bones of my body shook together.

The land fell silent on all sides. You could not hear a living thing, not close, not in the distance. Not dogs, not nighttime frogs, not even the coughing of a man. There was only one sound now for all our ears to hear: the fierce, pounding rain pouring down upon us all.

The next morning we passed the now-empty checkpoint on our way out. Blood from people who had been on the bus mixed in standing water at the crossing. People had no choice but to drive through. Those who had died in the bus still lay where they had fallen, the bus torn open. I felt the air, still thick with fear.

I called my daughter. "Go to the airport, Aker. Leave while you can!" There was only a little gunfire where she was now. "Your brother-in-law can pick you up."

She called me from his car later, stunned and scared. "Mother, there is so much blood out here. There are so many bodies." Nothing had prepared her for what she would see in the streets.

"No, Aker, don't look, don't look!"

"Mother, I can't stop looking."

It is a terrible thing when war steals forever your child's innocence.

Only one plane managed to land that day. Aker called me from the airport to tell me she was on it. It was the last plane to make it out of Juba to Nairobi. Three hours after she left, fighting revved up again. Calls were coming in on our phones, announcing this one was killed, that one was missing. A boy younger than my son was killed. That one, that boy, he used to call me auntie.

Oh, why, my dear Sudan, do you not love your children?

After three days of fighting there was a break for just one hour. We filled our bags with hard candy, powdered milk, hard biscuits, and peanut butter and took off for Konyo-Konyo, one of the few safe places left in the city. We hunkered down there for three weeks until finally good news came. The rebels and their leader Riek Machar, once again banished from government, had been driven out.

But our streets were still uneasy with grief. People had died not only from bullets but from heart attack and shock. The streets that once flowed with blood now flowed with processions of slow dance and low song for the beloved ones we had lost.

In wartime you learn to take small joys as treasures, whether it's sweet tea from a gentle friend, even when passed to you in a metal cup; the birth of a child, though by flashlight in a refugee tent; or a wedding in the midst of war. We decided to stay on in Juba with my sister and her fiancé. They were planning to get married soon. Their wedding would be a healing time for us all.

THE NEED FOR ANOTHER KIND OF HEALING WAS ALSO IN OUR HEARTS. After that night and more weeks of rebel fighting, many of us, all women, came together. The rebels had not only killed government soldiers, but also were targeting women, children, and even babies. They had stopped many buses, not just the one we saw. They set them on fire, killed the travelers. They halted traffic, looking for Dinka and when they found them pulled them from their cars, raping the women before killing them along with their families. Many victims you could no longer recognize after the rebels had cut them down.

This was a new level of violence to come within city walls. We knew it would spread out like a terrible sickness if we did nothing. Each woman among us took it to heart to find a way. We said, "This is no longer patriot against patriot. It is grudge against grudge. And now this targeted killing of women and children is the killing of our future."

So three women—Awut Deng, minister of gender and child welfare, Nyandeng Malek, former governor of Warrap, and Rachel Nyadak, known for her compassion as the "Mother of Widows"— called out to all women leaders everywhere in the nation. The call went out by phone, by publication, by word of mouth, to women from all groups, all tribes, all towns and cities, leaders from the highest to the most basic levels of responsibility, to women of all languages in South Sudan. The call went out for all women to speak with one voice, whether by coming together in Juba city or, if they could not come, by giving support from the towns where they were.

In less than the time it takes to draw breath and cry out, fifty of us came together in Juba to envision what would come next. I will name a few of these pioneer women, so that their actions will not be forgotten in history, as so often happens to the heroic deeds of the unnamed: Agnes Oswaha, first acting permanent representative of South Sudan to the United Nations, was among us in 2017, witnessing the carnage. Lily Akol, deputy minister of information and broadcasting, took notes with Agnes during the subsequent meeting with male heads of state, so that no word or promise could be forgotten. Akon Aldo Ajou, a British citizen who, like many, rushed back to South Sudan to help, worked with me to unite businesswomen in Juba. Nadia Dudi, whom I met as a convention delegate in 2008, now joined the campaign. Rebecca Joshua Okwaci, a woman who never gave way to her sadness, minister of telecommunications and postal services, who also spent time in Itang camp, joined in with her indomitable optimism.

Among us also were Yar Manoah, woman representative in the chamber of commerce; Salwa Bakony, vice president of the chamber of commerce; Naima Abbas, minister of gender and social welfare in Wau; Zainab Yasin, chairperson of Women's Association of South Sudan; Josephine Napwon, from Kapoeta Equatoria, minister of environment and forestry; Dr. Pauline Riak, chair of the board of directors of Sudd Institute (a place of independent research into public policy and practice) and vice chancellor of the University of Juba.

Nearly all were university graduates, with degrees in law, public policy, and the like. I had no degree. My schools had been the hospital in Ethiopia, the refugee camp in Itang, the narrow apartments of Nairobi, and the welcoming and sometimes unwelcoming US. It was in those hardship schools where I learned the great lesson that love for one another in community is the swiftest path toward peace.

Now, may the many more great women whose names I have not mentioned here forgive me as I move on to tell the story of all that happened next.

In our first meeting we decided to go, the fifty of us together, to each department of government, one office at a time. The officials were shocked when such a large troop of women appeared at their door to talk with them. The Minister of the Interior. The Office of the Vice President. The Ministry of Cabinet Affairs. The Office of the Chief of Security. The President's Chief of Staff. We also went area by area around Juba city, speaking to the women of each place. In those places there was often a local chief too; we spoke to each of them.

Then we chose Gudele as the place where everyone would meet. Over one thousand women, even men and youth, gathered in the open air. Our message to the women was that now that the killing had come against our children and ourselves, we must tell our husbands that this war must stop. That it was senseless and has no meaning. There was no need for even one South Sudanese to kill another South Sudanese.

A youth, born into war, who had known only strife his whole life, spoke up in front of all. "No good can come from this fight. We should sit down at the table and resolve our problems. In my lifetime, I want to know what it is like to live in peace!"

A musician joined us to sing about the strength of unity; he sang boldly that war is no good and must end. I stood and spoke too:

"Women and men of South Sudan: Unite! Tribalism has no value! We must stop fearing each other. We must stop hating each other. Unity is love. Unity is forgiveness. Forgiveness is peace.

"When there is peace, we can live and sell our goods to one another out in the open street. Today, you do not bring your produce to market and sit down, because you are afraid. When there is peace, you can sit down and sell all the food you have grown and all the good things you have made—openly, on every street, in every market, without fear. Many of us want to use our hands for good and not for war. So let us all unite for peace!"

People from all walks of life in South Sudan—Dinka, Nuer, Equatorian, Kakua, Madi, Taposa, Mundari, Shuluk, Jur Chol, and many other tribes and languages—all gathered together under the one sun that day in Juba. We spoke in Arabic so all the people could understand. There was shouting and applause. There was high song and joyful dancing, as each woman present took her turn at the mic to speak her mind.

This is our way, to give our time to one another, no matter how long. All spoke with one heart and one thought. So, we joined together in soul agreement that day as our vision for peace grew as bright as the sun.

Before we met that day in Gudele, we also met with the councils of elders of South Sudan, starting with the Jieng Council. They are not a government body, but a council of elders much respected in the Dinka community, important figures that the people appeal to for help solving problems. The Council was composed of mostly men and a handful of women. We found out that the Nuer council had accused these Dinka elders of giving false information to President Salva Kiir. This was a strong rumor among the Nuer. We told the Jieng Council that they were being blamed for the current conflict.

"This is what people are saying about you, and now people are being killed on the street. What is your position on this killing of women and children?"

We asked them to talk to the president, to tell him that the war had to stop. We asked them what part they would play in bringing peace to the country. The Council answered us at first by blaming the Nuer and the Equatorial councils. Then we talked to the Nuer elders in Juba, those in the office of the president, and to the Equatorial elders.

At first each elders' council blamed the other councils for the extended conflict, saying that when they invited the others to come talk, they didn't come. But separately and privately, the Equatorial, the Dinka, and the Nuer councils suggested that perhaps there should be a single Council of Elders, instead of three separate ones. When the Nuer and Equatorial Councils agreed to put that idea forward, we took it to the Dinka. The Dinka Council told us they were ready for it and said, "Let's meet."

They all needed to stop spreading rumors about each other.

So we sent word to the chiefs of the sixty-four diverse tribes of South Sudan, both those who would travel a long distance and those who were based in Juba. We called upon the chief of all the chiefs, and then he himself more strongly urged all sixty-four to come. The communication was unusually good in this case. The same message went out to each chief with no twists in it or shadows.

This had never happened before.

It fell to us to arrange a meeting place that could hold two thousand people. We chose Freedom Hall in Juba and set a date in November 2017.

We divided up the tasks: women who raised money to cover the costs, women who were the on-the-ground organizers, women in charge of communication, women who coordinated the different task groups together, and more. We labored without sleeping, with one purpose and heart; there was no strife or ambition, so the work moved the way small streams flow into a river. Waters, no matter where they are—in rivulets or rapids—all flow toward the sea, gather strength in their courses, and empty into the great waters as one.

Our love for our beautiful land flows this way.

We called all these people and many, many came to Freedom Hall —male chiefs and leaders and many women. But I felt fear when I entered that hall. The sound in the room was dark and loud, vibrating with the rumble of male voices raised like the growling of one lion against another. I knew that sound, I'd heard it in the bush outside the camp at Itang. I had escaped the lion then. I would make it now.

Agnes and Lily stood with courage, to silence the hall and moderate the meeting:

"Every man has to speak out his mind. If you want to come to peace and a lasting agreement, you must speak now all that is in your heart. Hide nothing."

At first, every group was pointing fingers at the others. As hour after hour of blaming raged on, the leading women managed to hold sway and at least kept the men speaking one after the other in order. But the finger-pointing continued. So some of our women decided they must intervene and stood up to speak their own mind, putting all the leaders in one basket together:

"Now we see who it is that is destroying South Sudan: All of you!" The scolding continued as the microphone passed from one angry woman to another.

At that moment an idea came to me: to give a gift to each of the men, to mark this moment when the gathering's direction turned. I searched to find someone who might have something to give. One said she had boxes of handkerchiefs for sale in her car. I asked her to bring them. And I stood to speak.

"Gentlemen, we will now give each of you a gift for you to remember this day and the great change you are about to make."

We handed out hundreds of white, embroidered handkerchiefs. I needed the men to understand that these small squares of white cloth, now in the hand of each, were not in any way white flags of defeat but were there to wipe the sweat off the brow of any man willing to do the hard work of peace.

"Now wipe away the sweat of conflict from your faces. Wipe away the war from your eyes and start fresh today," I told them.

Each man accepted the gift and used it immediately, for each man's face was indeed soaked in sweat from the long, hard hours of blaming.

Agnes held high a fist full of papers. "Every man's words are being written down. Think hard what you want to be remembered for."

Then we invited a leader from each tribe to the microphone to speak. Each would now be on record and under pressure to do what was best for all. This was each man's chance to save his country.

It lasted two days. Agnes and Lily produced a transcript from everything each leader said. Then, in front of everyone, they confirmed with each leader, "Is this what you just promised?" When each agreed, it became part of the record, so that no man could go back on his word.

Then we told them, "What we need from you now is for you to come to one agreement about this: What is the way forward now for our country?"

Together, the now-reconciled tribesmen hammered out a resolution. They agreed to have one single Council of Elders; they agreed on a National Peace Dialogue, like the truth and reconciliation councils of South Africa and Rwanda; and they agreed on the shared purpose of peace and unity. They also agreed to spread this word to the grassroots militia carrying out killings all over South Sudan. After

the resolution was signed, it was taken to the president, and he
formed the National Peace Dialogue in May 2018.

THE WHOLE COUNTRY WAS GIVEN A CHANCE TO SEE SOMETHING NEW
that day: when you want something done and done well for the good
of all, ask the women. In the news reports, however, not one of us is
mentioned. President Selva Kiir got full credit for creating the
National Peace Dialogue. This is the old Sudan way.

After the conference concluded, we were called immediately to
refugee concerns. Hundreds of internally displaced persons (IDP's),
mostly from the Nuer tribe, were in the UNMISS Camp in Juba. Nuer
advocates called Rachel and told her that now, since there was hope
of peace, the refugees in the UNMISS camp desired to go home but
could not. They feared the Dinka militia would kill them on the way.

Akon and I worked hard with business leaders to find money to
transport these people home, but their safety was much harder to
secure. We went to the military's chief of staff.

"Sir, the refugees are afraid to be killed when they leave the UN
camp to go home."

He said, "No, there will be no problem," and gave us his word.

"Sir, we will need military vehicles and a military escort to
protect them."

Again, he agreed.

"And, sir, we will need fuel for the vehicles."

Then he said, "No, we will not put gas in them. That will be your
problem."

So we searched for sponsors and negotiated a gasoline discount as
well. Then we had to find food that the Nuer refugees could take with
them. Lam Tungwar, former refugee and musician, now the minister
of information at the Nuer state of Liech, went to work with us,
offering to go with us to find the funds. His advisor went with us to
the markets and bought sacks of rice, sugar, salt, tea leaves, oil,

beans, and even powdered milk for the children. We rented a truck to bring back all he bought.

None of us slept. People would call us at any time, day or night, to tell us what they needed or what they had to give. We even bought airtime for the drivers to make calls to our headquarters along the way. Then we ourselves tracked the transports by phone, through the night. They called us whenever anything blocked them. One caravan called: "The tire is blown out and we are stranded." We mobilized help for them.

We moved a hundred and fifty refugees out safely the first time, seventy-five by seventy-five, in two trucks. The second time two trucks, again with seventy-five and seventy-five. Then the third time a volunteer gave us his cargo plane and received lines and lines of people into his plane, about a hundred and fifty people in all and all their baggage. Almost five hundred Nuer people were able to move out of the camp safely and go home. This continued until we ran out of money. By that time there were mostly only men left in the camp. The women and children had made it home. I returned to the US after that, once that stage of the process was complete.

But our work is still far from done. It continues from day to night to day again.

The work of peace is a personal thing and a community thing that must go on forever.

Abuk (right) with Finella Lam at a conference hosted by UN Women at the UN Compound in Nairobi, Kenya on October 2022.

EPILOGUE

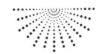

Until the lion learns to write, every story will glorify the hunter.

I HAVE TOLD YOU MY STORY AS I HAVE LIVED IT AND REMEMBER IT. At age sixteen, my son Dut—I call him David now—told me, "Mother, you have to write your story. People have to know." In this book I have fulfilled the wish of my once-dying child. We are okay now, myself and my three children. We are safe and sheltered, working in new countries, and our family is growing. But my beloved South Sudan is struggling still.

I am working alongside thousands of other women in South Sudan and throughout all the places where war has scattered us. We are working together to heal our country's heart, to bring harvests to desolated land, to teach trade and peace side-by-side. But while we are building, others are still tearing down. It is to the unfortunate ones, who know only to tear down, that we offer this message.

We are women. Our work has always stretched beyond the lines of sunrise and sunset. Do not think of us as weak because we do not fight by killing. We fight by giving birth to life, we fight by feeding the young from our own bodies, we raise up new life from our own ashes. For this, one must be stronger than death itself. We are such women. We are not victims, but proud bearers of the wisdom of generations, we are every country's lifeline of hope for the future.

Hear us, then, and learn from us. And let us love you and let us bring you back to peace.

—ABUK JERVAS MAKUAC

AFTERWORD

HOW ABUK AND I MET AND WORKED TOGETHER

ONE NIGHT IN 1999 WHILE I WAS HELPING IN A CLASS AT CATHOLIC Charities on Life Skills for the US, the leader split us into groups and placed me with Abuk and her son David, then 16 years old. As we went over the basic skills needed in retail positions, I asked her if she could read and write. At that point David stepped in and said I needed to know who I was talking to, who his mom was and all she had done in her life. The leader overheard and repeated to me what he had said and asked Abuk to confirm this, because the leader knew her. Abuk nodded. "I keep telling her she needs to write a book," her son said. But she scolded him, "I do not write well in English." At that point I said, "That doesn't matter. You talk. I'll type." And so it began.

We decided to meet at Abuk's apartment so I could tape her story. The first afternoon I was welcomed by her and her three teenage children, who greeted me with much kindness. Though it was light outside, her third-floor apartment patio was closed off by heavy floral curtains, making the apartment dark. Only later did I understand the great meaning and value of shade in Abuk's life. Large, well-used furniture overfilled the living room, which also served as a dining area, where a heavy wooden table and chair set stood. After a few hours of taping the first night, we had only scratched the surface.

We began to meet weekly as her story unfolded with so many twists and turns and so much beauty. Sometimes I brought fruit. Sometimes there was a meal prepared. As Abuk described to me the foods of Sudan, I ate them with her at the large table and learned how it was to share a meal in the Sudanese way. Sometimes old friends from the refugee camp would drop by and I watched how they talked and laughed together about the life they had in the camp. They asked me to write their books too. Abuk invited me to her church, where we danced while they sang and clapped and laughed more. We went to serious meetings together where the women lamented the economic and emotional state of their people back home and of the refugees here. For a time, Abuk and some of those women met regularly in my home to discuss leadership and democracy. Once I went with her to Kansas City to meet with 400 women to discuss the same. A few times some of the young men who had also lived in the camp visited Abuk while we were taping. They recounted their stories as well. Some of those stories are included in the book as scenes that mirror our gatherings on those nights. A few times I also met with some of the men who had fought in the war, who had been leaders in the fight. They were cordial, but in those meetings, I felt what it was to have the air sucked out of me, to touch the death they carried with them.

Over the course of our twenty-year interaction Abuk's children graduated from high school, attended college, married, had children. Abuk herself periodically returned to Sudan to care for her mother and to meet with women there. During those times we would lose touch and our work would be suspended. Eventually, as technology advanced to the point where it is today, we were better able to find each other. Over the last few years, I've witnessed her live-streaming over Facebook and interacting with expatriates from all over the world, trying to persuade others of the value of dialogue and of peace. One night as I watched her live stream in Arabic internationally over the small phone in her hand, passionately speaking and debating for over an hour and patiently listening as a man disagreed with her, her son said to me, "You don't know my mom like I do. In Arabic she is eloquent and powerful. In English..." he shrugged his shoulders.

In 2019 we met to read the finished chapters together over tea and rice in her youngest daughter's apartment in Dallas. Abuk herself no longer has a fixed home. Those evenings sometimes I read out loud. Sometimes her son did, checking every scene and word for truthfulness and tone. And now finally, in 2022, we have finished the last chapter over the internet while Abuk is in Juba with her oldest daughter. She returns to the US in August. Now we hope the book will be published and be able to do its work in the world.

—SUSAN LYNN CLARK
Dallas, Texas, 2022

ACKNOWLEDGMENTS

I have to start by thanking my friend Susan Clark. This book would not have been possible if it weren't for her dedication, hard work and incredible patience. Her commitment to helping me tell my story leaves me speechless.

Our friendship was formed twenty-plus years ago and since then Susan has been an integral part of my family's life. She helped buy my daughter's violin when she was a freshman in high school, helped my son contribute artwork for a comic book about the lost boys of South Sudan, and finally she has always communed with us in our home. She is more than a friend to me and my family, and I will be eternally grateful to her.

To my late husband, George Maker Benjamin, thank you for encouraging me to write this book and tell our story. Even though our life together has had many struggles, we always remember that the foundation of our marriage was built upon our friendship. Not only were you my husband but you were my best friend. I miss you dearly and wish you were here to read this book about our lives.

To my cousin and longtime friend, Awut Deng Aculi, the Honourable Minister of Education, thank you for your unwavering support. Anytime I've come to you with an idea or advice you have always supported me. Your encouragement is very much appreciated and I feel very blessed to have you on my side.

Finally to Judy Blankenship and Anne McClard of Aristata Press, thank you for your assistance in bringing this book together. This wouldn't have been possible without your help.

—ABUK JERVAS MAKUAC

ABOUT THE AUTHORS

ABUK JERVAS MAKUAC was born in Rumbek, South Sudan in 1962. Soon after the civil war ignited in 1983, she and her husband and young son were forced to leave their middle-class life in Southern Sudan. *Women Caught in the Crossfire* traces her perilous flight, surviving an overcrowded refugee camp in Ethiopia, living in hiding in Kenya, and eventually resettling in the US. Deeply convinced that peace is a basic need and the right of every human being, Makuac has spoken on behalf of South Sudanese women and children on many platforms throughout the world. In the US, she founded the Women's Movement Against War, served as Chairperson for the Women's League of the Sudanese People's Liberation Movement, and is currently Chairperson of the Chamber of Women Entrepreneurs in Southern Sudan.

SUSAN LYNN CLARK holds a doctorate in humanities and a masters in linguistics, with a special focus on trauma and resilience in immigrant and refugee populations. Since 1984 Dr. Clark has worked with immigrants and refugees in the US, helping with access to higher education and teaching language and survival skills. She currently works as a licensed psychotherapist in Fort Worth, Texas in a clinic for underserved populations. Previously, she served in New York following 9/11, in El Paso, Texas with unaccompanied minors from Central America, and on medical missions in Honduras where she provided continuing education in remote areas affected by decades of violent unrest.

SELECT ARISTATA PRESS TITLES

LEAVINGS: Memoir of a 1920s Hollywood Love Child, by Megan McClard, 2022

Díganle a mi madre que estoy en el paraíso: Memorias de una prisionera política en El Salvador, by Ana Margarita Gasteazoro, edited by Judy Blankenship and Andrew Wilson, 2022. Spanish language edition of *Tell Mother I'm in Paradise: Memoirs of a Political Prisoner in El Salvador,* University of Alabama Press, 2022.

COMING IN 2023

This Rough Magic: At Home on the Columbia Slough, by Nancy Henry and Bruce Campbell, illustrated by Amanda Williams, August 2023.

Butterfly Dreams: a Novel, by Anne McClard, August 2023.

Women Caught in the Crossfire: One Woman's Quest for Peace in South Sudan, by Abuk Jervas Makuac and Susan Lynn Clark, October 2023.

Raising Owen: an Extra-ordinary Memoir on Motherhood, by Suzanne Lezotte, October 2023.

Aristata Press is non-profit organization. We depend on charitable contributions and volunteers to keep the lights on. We are a tax exempt–501(c)(3)–organization (EIN 92-0281706), which means that your contributions are tax deductible. Contributions that we receive will go directly to supporting the publications of deserving literary works by authors that for one reason or another would be unlikely to find a home in the for-profit publishing sector.

Please visit us at: https://aristatapress.com

Printed in the USA
CPSIA information can be obtained
at www.ICGtesting.com
LVHW031931090923
757555LV00023B/44/J